The MOON DIVAS ORACLE

WISDOM & WONDER AND THE POWER OF PLACE

by LARA VESTA

First Printing: 2017

ISBN 978-1-365-74018-3

Giantess Press
www.veleda.org
veledavest@gmail.com

Ordering Information:

Special discounts are available on quantity purchases by corporations, associations, educators, and others. For details, contact the publisher at the above listed address.

U.S. trade bookstores and wholesalers: Please contact Giantess Press or email lara@laravesta.co.

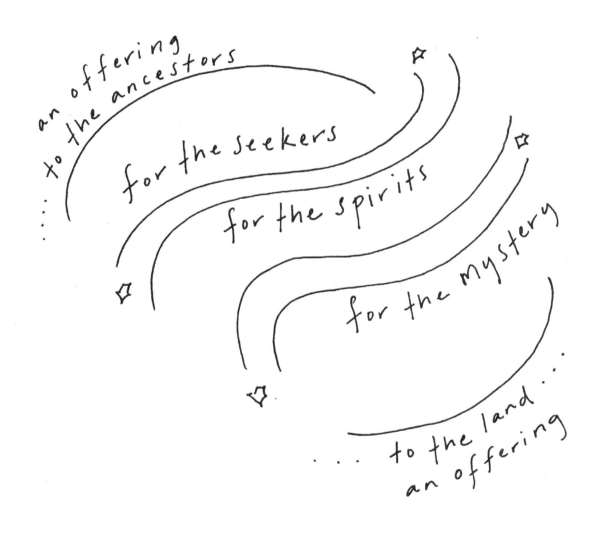

an offering
to the ancestors
...

for the seekers

for the spirits

for the mystery

... to the land ...
an offering

The Moon Divas Oracle
A Map

The Beginning Place

This oracle deck began in a hazelnut orchard on the edge of Forest Grove, Oregon in 2008. It was early summer and I worked mornings in a cubicle on a contract-writing job. When I had finished my copy for the day, I would ride my bike out to the cemetery and from there, as Mary Oliver says, enter the kingdom. The orchard welcomed me with a shiver of green leaves, archways that held the wind and framed view after view of farmlands and mountains.

Every day for months I spent my time in the orchard, mostly in prayer. My life was in crisis. I was a single mom, parenting long distance, separated from my children for fourteen days each month. I was an adjunct professor of writing at the local university, a dog walker and a freelancer trying to make enough money to survive. I lived in a small bedroom in another woman's home. I was involved in a love relationship that was out of integrity and tearing me apart. Only in the orchard did I find ease and acceptance. It was practice that opened me to possibilities, prayer that helped me feel at home even in the chaos of my days.

In the orchard I prayed to release what was no longer serving me, I prayed to open to new and positive ways of being. I prayed to live my purpose, even though struggle. The trees answered, always answered, the wind carrying their song.

One day in the orchard, I found a tree with a limb just right for sitting. I rested in the crook of that tree and allowed it to rock me with the winds gusting up off the wheat below, thistledown filling the air. A kestrel flew circles and called to me. I realized, with a welling in my heart, that I was a part of everything there. In that moment the spirits of the land, the trees, the animals all reassured me that I belonged. That whatever happened in my human life there was something in me beyond my problems, something intrinsic and ancient that ran through everything and all.

This oracle deck reflects my moment of synchronicity, the divine expressed in substance, in universal concepts, in the elements, and personified in visage by the feminine. From these forms, because we are so elaborately a part of the world we live in, we can draw wisdom.

Release . . . Receive

Whenever I offer a reading for someone I always say, "there's nothing in these cards that doesn't already live within you." From this place of union, we open, ready to receive information from the universal unconscious.

That information comes in the form of symbols. This is where our conscious mind goes to work, decoding spiritual information into conscious language.

In my time of transition over the past ten years I've used a lot of oracles to access spiritual guidance. The impulse to create one of my own came from collaborative work with Ingrid Kincaid, the Rune Woman. Together we made two decks, the *(un)familiar Runic Journey Deck* and *The Lost Teachings of the North: The Runes, the Wheel and the Tree*. These decks align with my spiritual path and my ancestry. But I wanted to make something uniquely feminine, something that would open

information for those drawn to the work of *The Moon Divas Guidebook*. I began with the Guidebook Goddesses, crafting *The Goddess Coloring Book and Self-Care Planner* in 2012. In 2013 I began drawing a Goddess series that would become The Goddesses of Portland, Oregon, a revolutionary project defining spirit in place. But the card deck really found its form when I created the Thirteen Days of Self-Care practice at the end of 2014. Those words and concepts, combined with the Goddesses, the Soul Directions and Gaia cards felt finally complete.

This work makes use of a spiritual concept called UPG, or Unverified Personal Gnosis. UPG supposes that we all have the ability to directly access spiritual information. So many of our ancestral cultures and traditions have been spiritually decimated, we have only fragments of threads with which to weave a whole. Not only this, but many of us are a rich combination of ethnic and cultural lineages. If we want to connect with the ways of our ancestors, whose do we choose?

Whatever your approach, this work requires your openness and willingness to receive, to access the unique interpretation that comes through only you. Don't rely simply on my words or the *Oracle Map*. This is a beginning place, but as you become familiar with the deck, allow yourself the freedom to put the *Map* away and listen to your own deep knowing.

Thank you for being a part of this story, this co-creative endeavor of wisdom work. May these cards bring you joy, clarify your purpose, and allow you to bring your gifts to the world.

I wish you love in the journey—

HOW TO USE THIS DECK

☆ ☆

1. Center: find a quiet space. Take three deep breaths. Imagine you are a tree. Feel the earth below you, the sky above.

☆ **2. Shuffle the cards.** ☆ As you shuffle, think on your question. I like to ask: what is the most important information I need in my life at this moment.

☆ **3. Lay out the cards face** ☆ down using the Moon Divas Spread or your favorite. As you turn the cards over, let your intuition guide the meaning. ♡♡♡

MORE INFORMATION @ laravesta.co

This is the quick reference version... for when you are ready...

...and not in the mood for at-length instructions...

you will find this card in the Oracle Deck for on-the-go consultation...

How to Use This Deck
(narrative version with notes)

All decks can be used casually, on the run, with a one card, "What do I most need to know?" pull. And this works fine in a hurry, but for the best and most complete results, set aside some time where you won't be disturbed and create sacred space. For more information on creating ritual space, see *The Moon Divas Guidebook*.

Once you have set ritual space, form a question. This should not be a yes or no question. I usually ask, "What do I most need to know right now to act for the highest good in this situation?" or "What should I focus on in the coming weeks?"

Readings are not permanent. They are a snapshot, a paused moment. In a series of snapshots, some things stay the same, some things are ever moving and changing. I usually say readings are good for about one moon phase. Then it is time to check in again. If you are in a particularly interesting place in your life with a lot of upheaval, you may want to read more often to align yourself with what is working through you.

**A note of caution on reading often: the divine is not to be trifled with. If you don't like the answer you receive from the cards, or keep asking the same question over and over again, the energies can get impatient and wisdom will be obscured.

You can read your cards in infinite ways, and are welcome to craft the way that works best for you. I like to read with this deck either in the one card pull mentioned above, as a past-present-future three-card spread, to get an overview of the situation, or by using the Moon Divas Oracle Spread to receive a depth perspective on my query.

Also, a few other ideas:
- develop a regular time and place for readings
- consider readings timed with natural rhythms - lunar, solar, earth
- record your readings in a notebook or use the reading pages in the back of this Map for reflection.

The Moon Divas Oracle Spread

6 — Source of Focus

4 — Guiding Principle

7 — Source of Support

2 — Past Reality

3 — Future Vision

8 — Divine Message

1 — Current Reality

9 — Possible Outcome

5 — Hidden Need

The Moon Divas Oracle Spread

1. Current Reality
This card represents the influences of the present moment, including your attitude and state of mind.

2. Past Realities
This card holds a quality of the past, and represents the influences of the past in regard to the situation you are asking about.

3. Future Vision
This card represents the potential of the future, as envisioned by you or by divinity in relationship to you.

4. Guiding Principle
The guiding principle is the overall theme of the reading. This is the element or symbol that will guide an outcome to the highest good.

5. Hidden Need
This is a source of sustenance and security, something that must be invoked or addressed in order for all to unfold as it needs to.

6. Source of Focus
This card represents a quality that can enhance and hone concentration toward the achievement of a goal or positive outcome.

7. Source of Support
This card represents something you can turn to in order to receive material or spiritual support through the unfolding of your process.

8. Divine Message
This is what the divine has to say about the element in question and your relationship to it.

9. Possible Outcome
The future is always changing depending on our attitudes and energies. This card is a read on one possible resolution to your current query if things keep moving along without substantial alteration.

If you feel confused by the 9th card, center and draw three more as "steps" to your possible outcome.

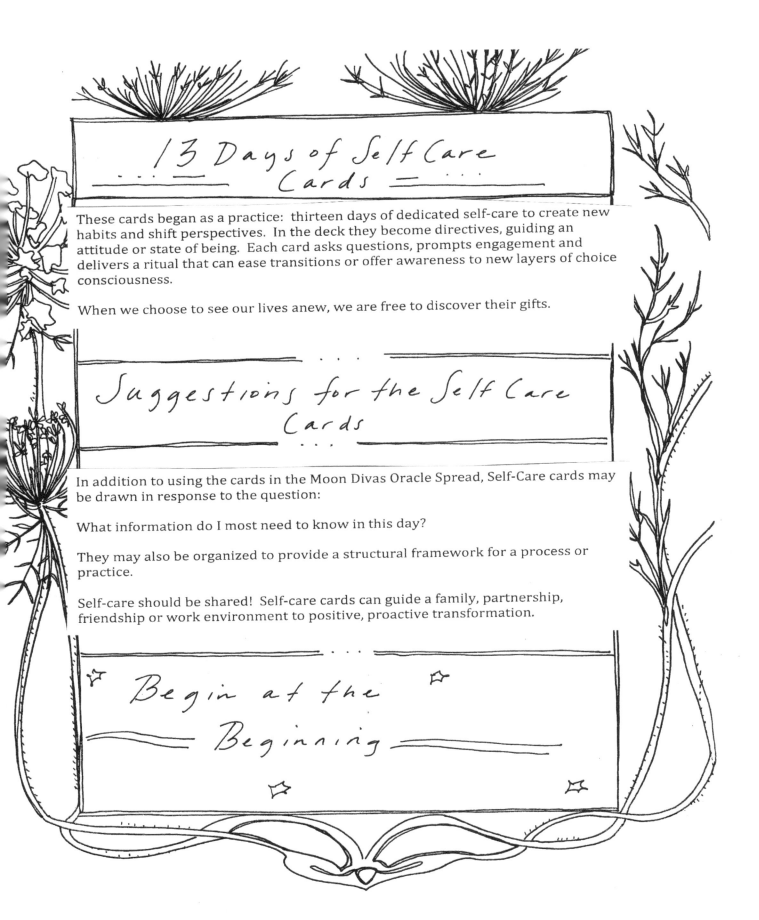

13 Days of Self Care Cards

These cards began as a practice: thirteen days of dedicated self-care to create new habits and shift perspectives. In the deck they become directives, guiding an attitude or state of being. Each card asks questions, prompts engagement and delivers a ritual that can ease transitions or offer awareness to new layers of choice consciousness.

When we choose to see our lives anew, we are free to discover their gifts.

Suggestions for the Self Care Cards

In addition to using the cards in the Moon Divas Oracle Spread, Self-Care cards may be drawn in response to the question:

What information do I most need to know in this day?

They may also be organized to provide a structural framework for a process or practice.

Self-care should be shared! Self-care cards can guide a family, partnership, friendship or work environment to positive, proactive transformation.

Begin at the Beginning

INTENTION

Did you know that you are worthy of your own love?
Did you know that you are already enough, right now, just as you are in this moment?

Today, stand with your hands over your heart.

Today, say:

I love myself.
I love myself without alteration.
I love who I am and what I do.
I love my body.
I love my story.
I love my life.
As it is now, with all of its imperfections. I accept where I am with love.

From the place of this affirmation, form an intention for your year ahead. What would you like to achieve?

Write it down. What about two years ahead? Write it. Five years? Yes, you guessed it. Write.

When you love and approve of yourself, there is nothing you cannot do.

In yourself, believe.

notes:

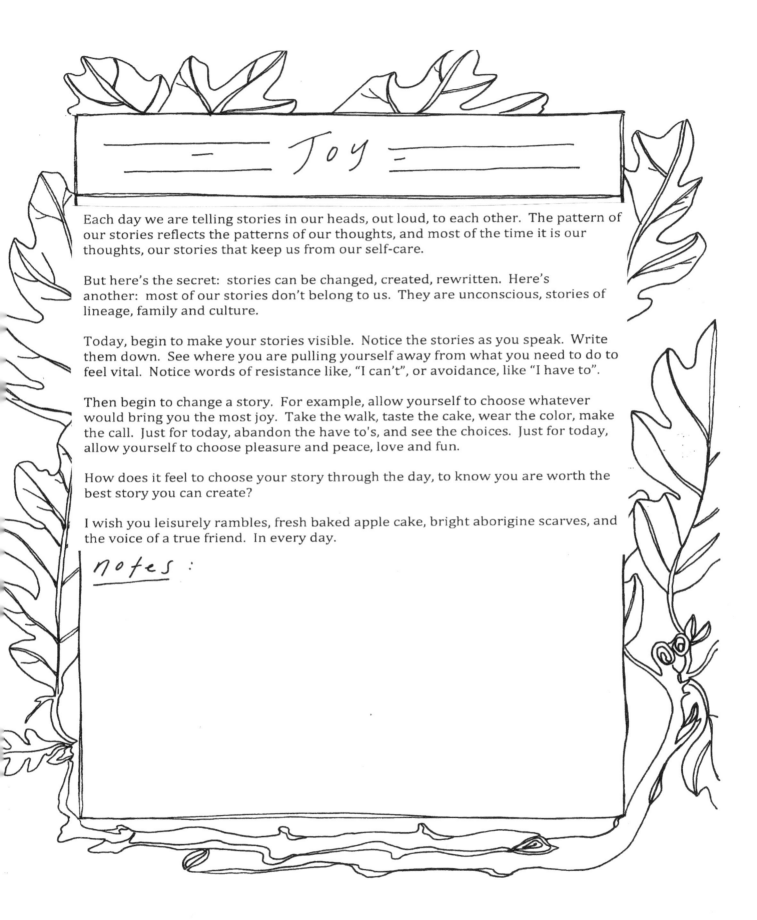

Joy

Each day we are telling stories in our heads, out loud, to each other. The pattern of our stories reflects the patterns of our thoughts, and most of the time it is our thoughts, our stories that keep us from our self-care.

But here's the secret: stories can be changed, created, rewritten. Here's another: most of our stories don't belong to us. They are unconscious, stories of lineage, family and culture.

Today, begin to make your stories visible. Notice the stories as you speak. Write them down. See where you are pulling yourself away from what you need to do to feel vital. Notice words of resistance like, "I can't", or avoidance, like "I have to".

Then begin to change a story. For example, allow yourself to choose whatever would bring you the most joy. Take the walk, taste the cake, wear the color, make the call. Just for today, abandon the have to's, and see the choices. Just for today, allow yourself to choose pleasure and peace, love and fun.

How does it feel to choose your story through the day, to know you are worth the best story you can create?

I wish you leisurely rambles, fresh baked apple cake, bright aborigine scarves, and the voice of a true friend. In every day.

notes:

MOTHER

Each of us, whatever our station, our gender, our race, religion or creed, was born from the womb of a mother. After our birth, the relationship with our biological mothers can become more complex. But when we trace our lineage through our bodies, we can remember that feeling of being held, of gentleness and peaceful receiving. We can begin to mother ourselves.

Consider your relationship with the mother: your own, or your role as a mother, or the archetype of the mother, or the great mother, as goddess divine. Amid the bustle of daily chores and expectations, take a moment to receive nourishment from yourself. In simple ways, a pause before eating, a candle lit, a written word, honor yourself as you honor the mother, from whom we all are born.

See if you can find, in relationship with yourself, a reservoir of deep and unconditional love.

notes :

GRATITUDE

May you realize you have everything you want.
May you know that everything you seek is inside you, gorgeous, accessible whenever you wish.

Thank you for being amazing.
Thank you for your beauty.
Thank you for all of your gifts.
Thank you for all you offer, and your ability to receive.
Thank you for being exactly who you are.
Thank you for believing in what you are becoming
even if you can't see the end
even if the road is dark.
Thank you for the trust, the chance, the risk, the fullness by which you live.
And today, let this gratitude be a superpower.
Let it transform from wanting to existing every bit of your sacred life.
You are enough, you do enough. More than enough.
You are.

Now find a quiet place in front of a mirror or glass or pool of water, and say these words to yourself today. Believe in your superpower.

notes:

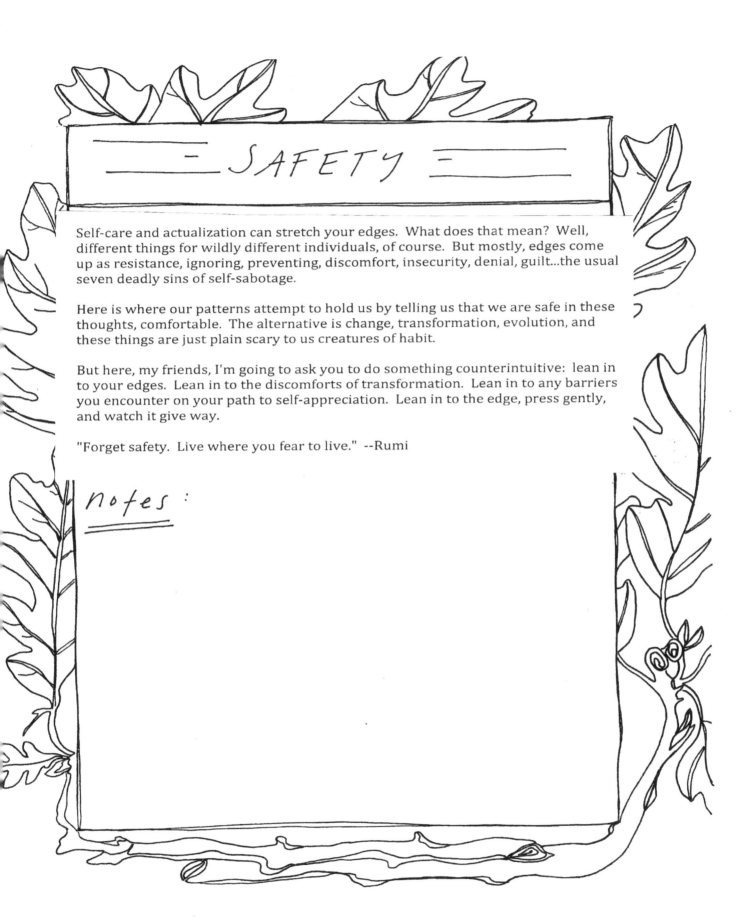

= SAFETY =

Self-care and actualization can stretch your edges. What does that mean? Well, different things for wildly different individuals, of course. But mostly, edges come up as resistance, ignoring, preventing, discomfort, insecurity, denial, guilt...the usual seven deadly sins of self-sabotage.

Here is where our patterns attempt to hold us by telling us that we are safe in these thoughts, comfortable. The alternative is change, transformation, evolution, and these things are just plain scary to us creatures of habit.

But here, my friends, I'm going to ask you to do something counterintuitive: lean in to your edges. Lean in to the discomforts of transformation. Lean in to any barriers you encounter on your path to self-appreciation. Lean in to the edge, press gently, and watch it give way.

"Forget safety. Live where you fear to live." --Rumi

notes:

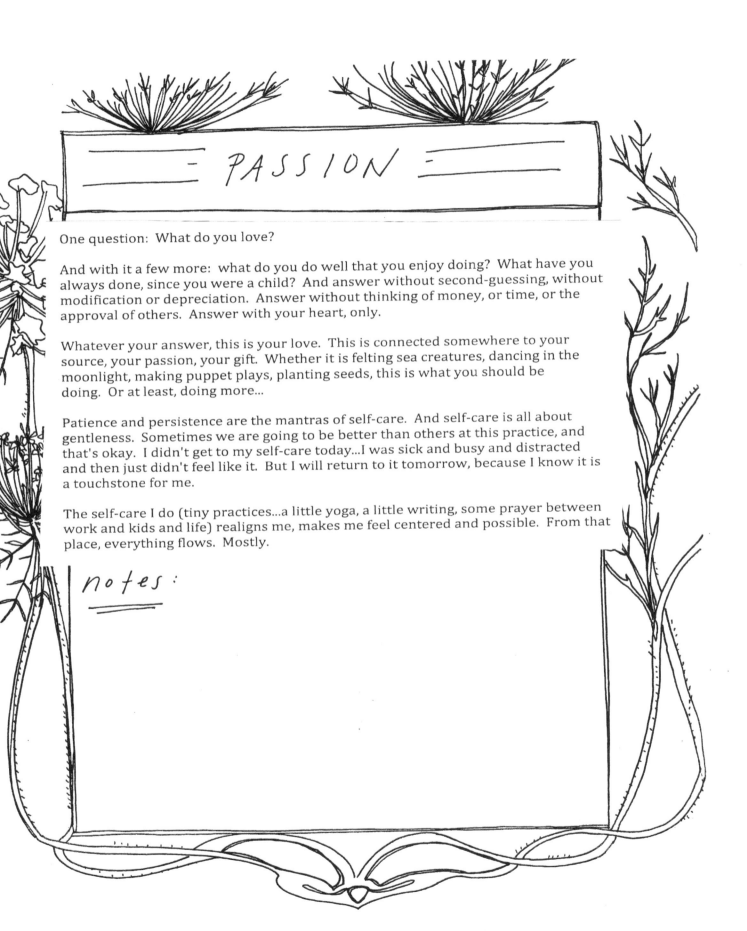

PASSION

One question: What do you love?

And with it a few more: what do you do well that you enjoy doing? What have you always done, since you were a child? And answer without second-guessing, without modification or depreciation. Answer without thinking of money, or time, or the approval of others. Answer with your heart, only.

Whatever your answer, this is your love. This is connected somewhere to your source, your passion, your gift. Whether it is felting sea creatures, dancing in the moonlight, making puppet plays, planting seeds, this is what you should be doing. Or at least, doing more...

Patience and persistence are the mantras of self-care. And self-care is all about gentleness. Sometimes we are going to be better than others at this practice, and that's okay. I didn't get to my self-care today...I was sick and busy and distracted and then just didn't feel like it. But I will return to it tomorrow, because I know it is a touchstone for me.

The self-care I do (tiny practices...a little yoga, a little writing, some prayer between work and kids and life) realigns me, makes me feel centered and possible. From that place, everything flows. Mostly.

notes:

PERSISTENCE

The key is persistence.

There is no judgment,
no grade,
no gold star.

Begin again at any time.

And on the days you can, add a little extra, more of what you love,
more joy,
more rest,
more fun.

notes:

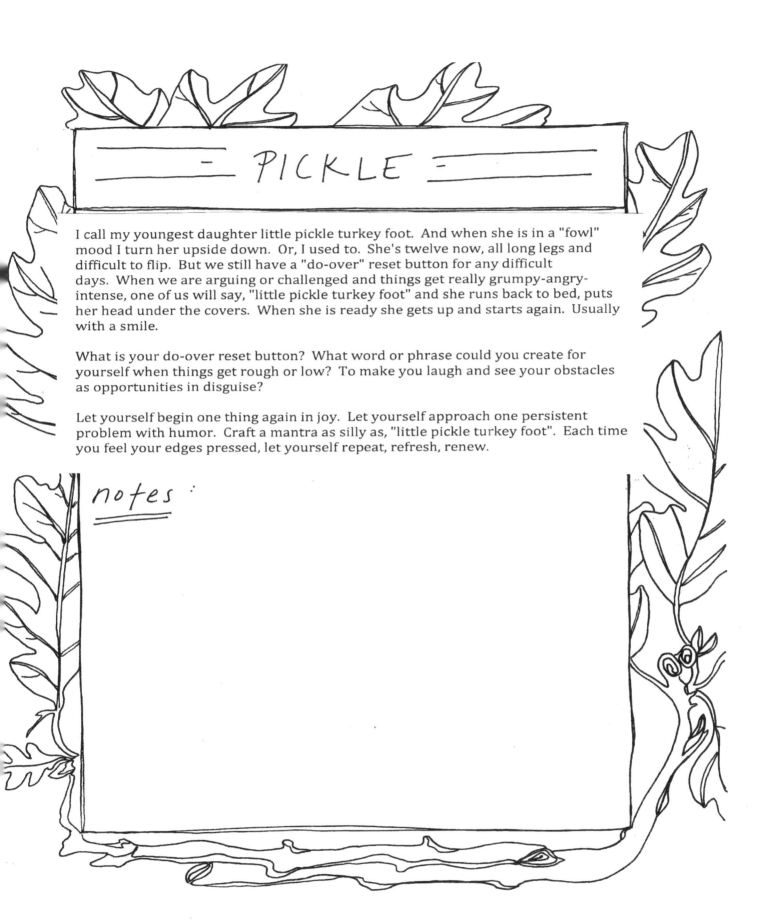

PICKLE

I call my youngest daughter little pickle turkey foot. And when she is in a "fowl" mood I turn her upside down. Or, I used to. She's twelve now, all long legs and difficult to flip. But we still have a "do-over" reset button for any difficult days. When we are arguing or challenged and things get really grumpy-angry-intense, one of us will say, "little pickle turkey foot" and she runs back to bed, puts her head under the covers. When she is ready she gets up and starts again. Usually with a smile.

What is your do-over reset button? What word or phrase could you create for yourself when things get rough or low? To make you laugh and see your obstacles as opportunities in disguise?

Let yourself begin one thing again in joy. Let yourself approach one persistent problem with humor. Craft a mantra as silly as, "little pickle turkey foot". Each time you feel your edges pressed, let yourself repeat, refresh, renew.

notes:

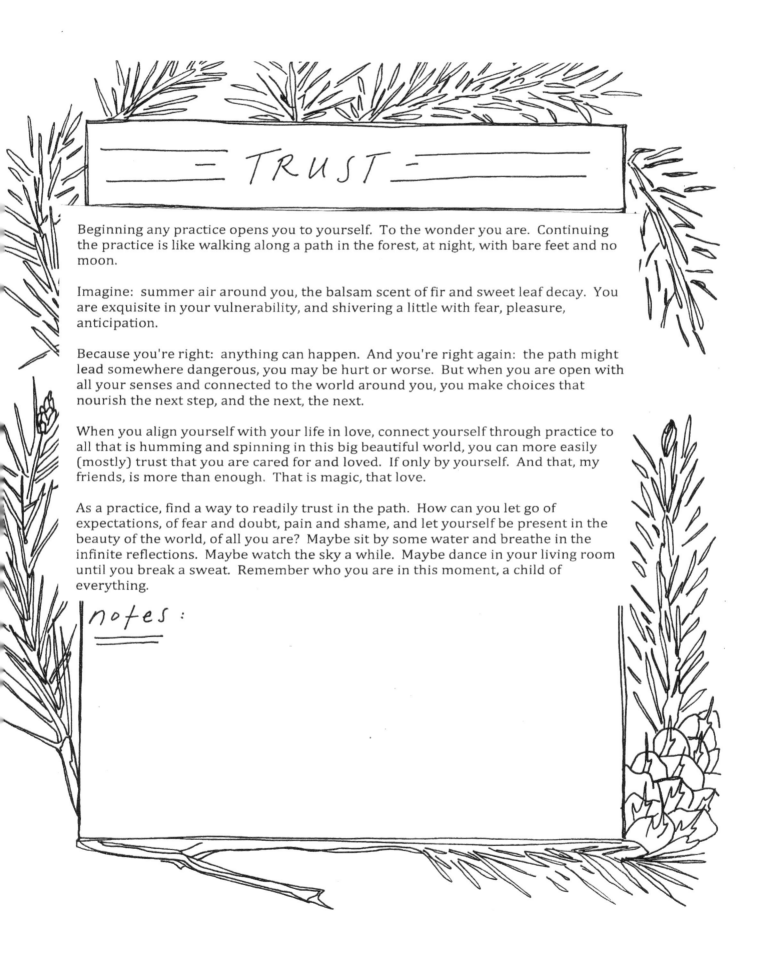

= TRUST =

Beginning any practice opens you to yourself. To the wonder you are. Continuing the practice is like walking along a path in the forest, at night, with bare feet and no moon.

Imagine: summer air around you, the balsam scent of fir and sweet leaf decay. You are exquisite in your vulnerability, and shivering a little with fear, pleasure, anticipation.

Because you're right: anything can happen. And you're right again: the path might lead somewhere dangerous, you may be hurt or worse. But when you are open with all your senses and connected to the world around you, you make choices that nourish the next step, and the next, the next.

When you align yourself with your life in love, connect yourself through practice to all that is humming and spinning in this big beautiful world, you can more easily (mostly) trust that you are cared for and loved. If only by yourself. And that, my friends, is more than enough. That is magic, that love.

As a practice, find a way to readily trust in the path. How can you let go of expectations, of fear and doubt, pain and shame, and let yourself be present in the beauty of the world, of all you are? Maybe sit by some water and breathe in the infinite reflections. Maybe watch the sky a while. Maybe dance in your living room until you break a sweat. Remember who you are in this moment, a child of everything.

notes:

- - NEW =

What can you see right now for the first time? I had a friend in college who would call to me from across the apartment, "Back away from the mirror!" She knew I was close in, analyzing my imperfections. For today, step back and view your accomplishments, your beauty, your sass and fascinating self with new eyes. See yourself as a stranger might see you. See yourself as the divine sees you, from that far away, as the totally unique and only you you are.

Then write yourself a letter from this vantage point. A love letter, from a viewer afar, an admirer or the divine. What can you say to yourself from a distance? How self-full can you be?

notes:

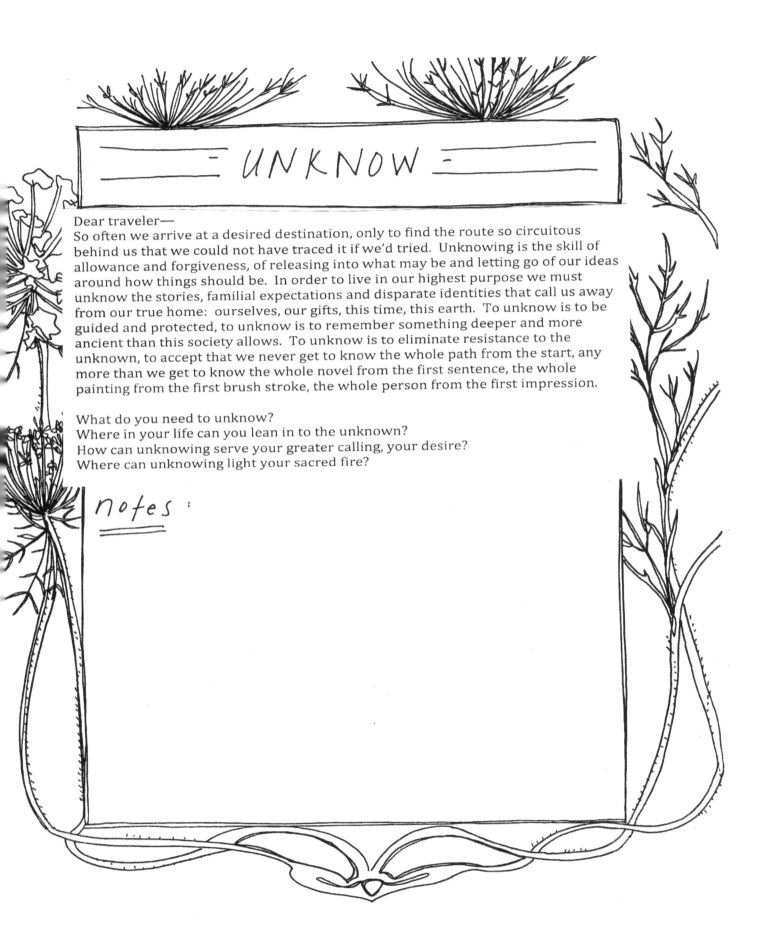

UNKNOW

Dear traveler—

So often we arrive at a desired destination, only to find the route so circuitous behind us that we could not have traced it if we'd tried. Unknowing is the skill of allowance and forgiveness, of releasing into what may be and letting go of our ideas around how things should be. In order to live in our highest purpose we must unknow the stories, familial expectations and disparate identities that call us away from our true home: ourselves, our gifts, this time, this earth. To unknow is to be guided and protected, to unknow is to remember something deeper and more ancient than this society allows. To unknow is to eliminate resistance to the unknown, to accept that we never get to know the whole path from the start, any more than we get to know the whole novel from the first sentence, the whole painting from the first brush stroke, the whole person from the first impression.

What do you need to unknow?
Where in your life can you lean in to the unknown?
How can unknowing serve your greater calling, your desire?
Where can unknowing light your sacred fire?

notes:

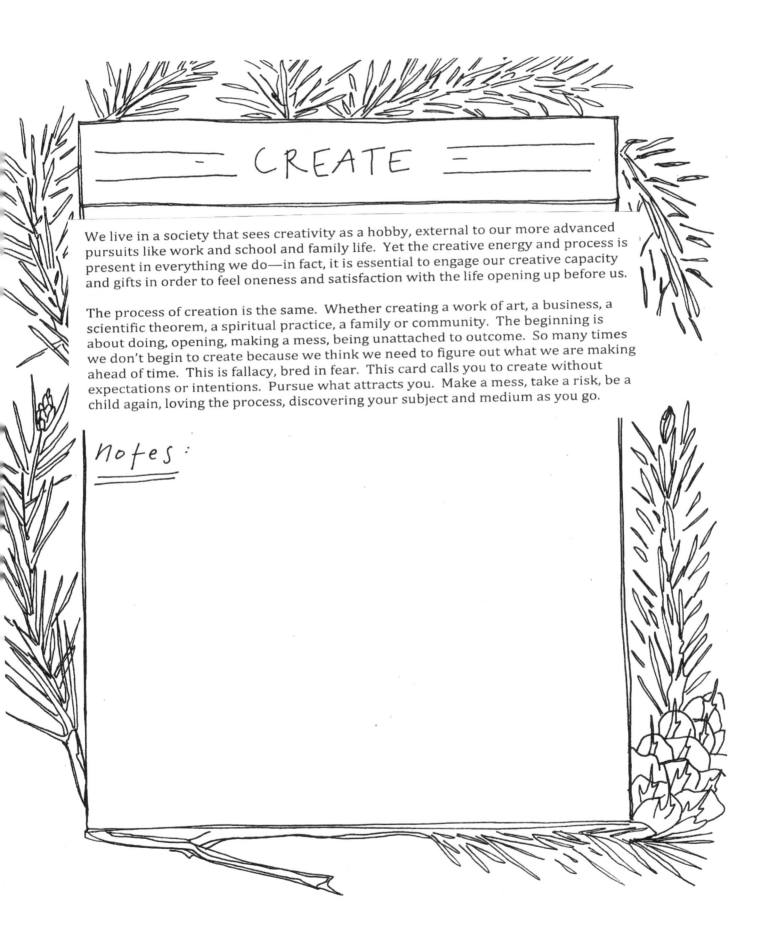

CREATE

We live in a society that sees creativity as a hobby, external to our more advanced pursuits like work and school and family life. Yet the creative energy and process is present in everything we do—in fact, it is essential to engage our creative capacity and gifts in order to feel oneness and satisfaction with the life opening up before us.

The process of creation is the same. Whether creating a work of art, a business, a scientific theorem, a spiritual practice, a family or community. The beginning is about doing, opening, making a mess, being unattached to outcome. So many times we don't begin to create because we think we need to figure out what we are making ahead of time. This is fallacy, bred in fear. This card calls you to create without expectations or intentions. Pursue what attracts you. Make a mess, take a risk, be a child again, loving the process, discovering your subject and medium as you go.

notes:

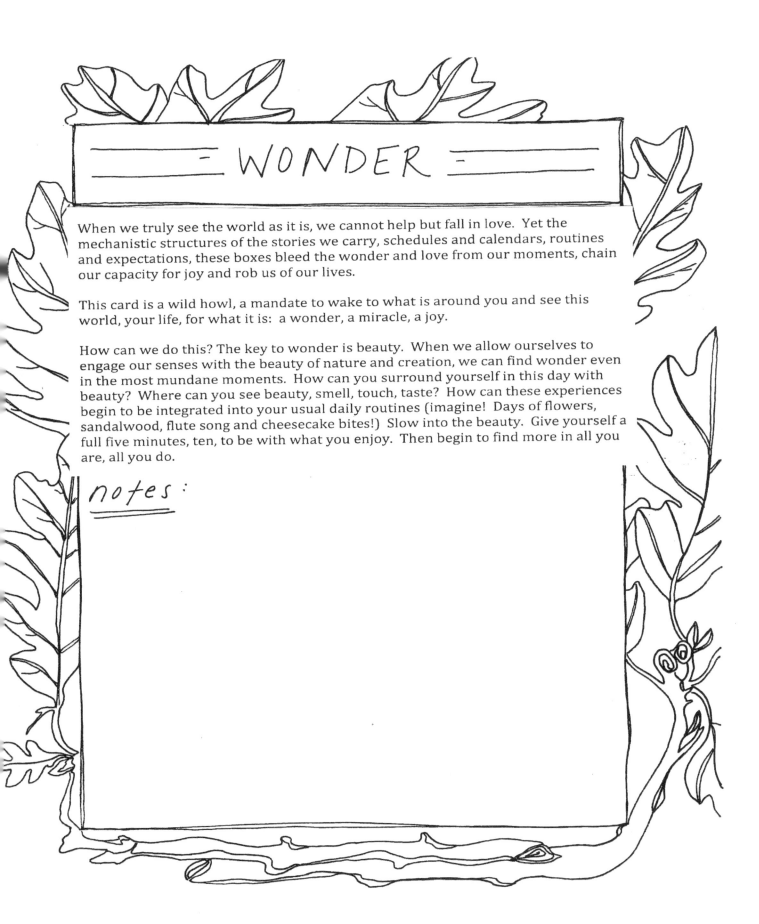

WONDER

When we truly see the world as it is, we cannot help but fall in love. Yet the mechanistic structures of the stories we carry, schedules and calendars, routines and expectations, these boxes bleed the wonder and love from our moments, chain our capacity for joy and rob us of our lives.

This card is a wild howl, a mandate to wake to what is around you and see this world, your life, for what it is: a wonder, a miracle, a joy.

How can we do this? The key to wonder is beauty. When we allow ourselves to engage our senses with the beauty of nature and creation, we can find wonder even in the most mundane moments. How can you surround yourself in this day with beauty? Where can you see beauty, smell, touch, taste? How can these experiences begin to be integrated into your usual daily routines (imagine! Days of flowers, sandalwood, flute song and cheesecake bites!) Slow into the beauty. Give yourself a full five minutes, ten, to be with what you enjoy. Then begin to find more in all you are, all you do.

notes:

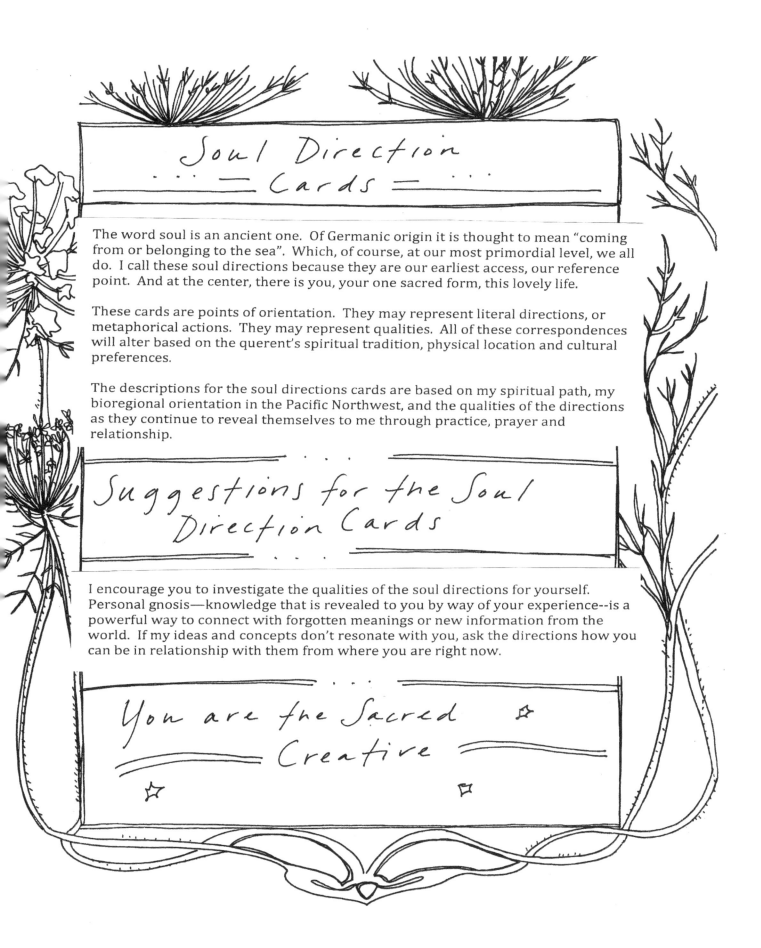

Soul Direction Cards

The word soul is an ancient one. Of Germanic origin it is thought to mean "coming from or belonging to the sea". Which, of course, at our most primordial level, we all do. I call these soul directions because they are our earliest access, our reference point. And at the center, there is you, your one sacred form, this lovely life.

These cards are points of orientation. They may represent literal directions, or metaphorical actions. They may represent qualities. All of these correspondences will alter based on the querent's spiritual tradition, physical location and cultural preferences.

The descriptions for the soul directions cards are based on my spiritual path, my bioregional orientation in the Pacific Northwest, and the qualities of the directions as they continue to reveal themselves to me through practice, prayer and relationship.

Suggestions for the Soul Direction Cards

I encourage you to investigate the qualities of the soul directions for yourself. Personal gnosis—knowledge that is revealed to you by way of your experience--is a powerful way to connect with forgotten meanings or new information from the world. If my ideas and concepts don't resonate with you, ask the directions how you can be in relationship with them from where you are right now.

You are the Sacred Creative

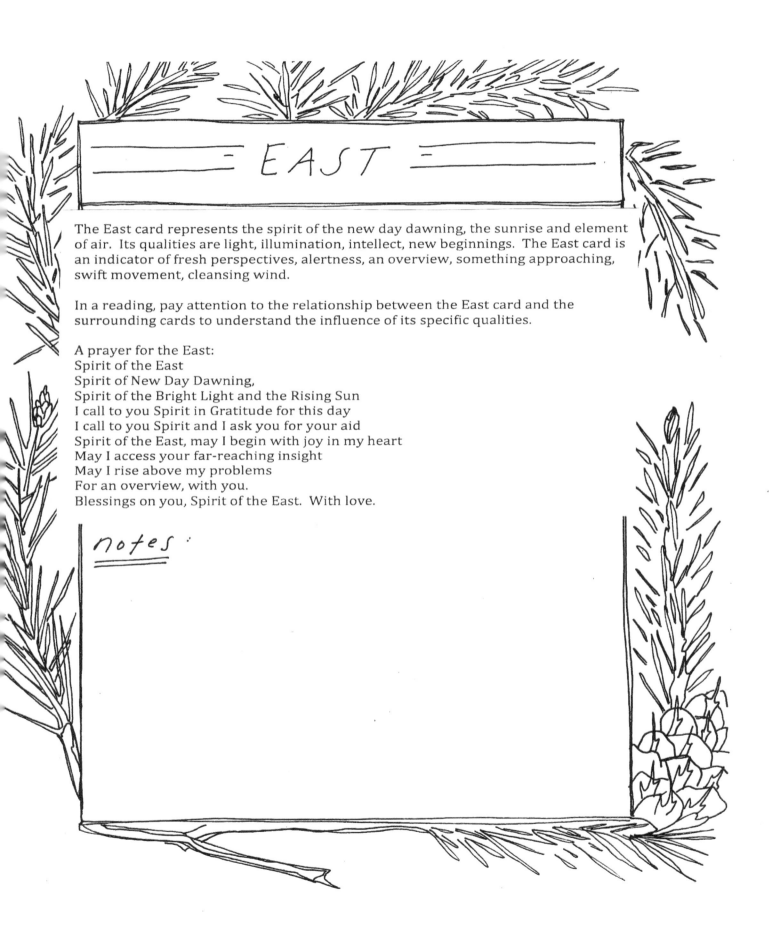

EAST

The East card represents the spirit of the new day dawning, the sunrise and element of air. Its qualities are light, illumination, intellect, new beginnings. The East card is an indicator of fresh perspectives, alertness, an overview, something approaching, swift movement, cleansing wind.

In a reading, pay attention to the relationship between the East card and the surrounding cards to understand the influence of its specific qualities.

A prayer for the East:
Spirit of the East
Spirit of New Day Dawning,
Spirit of the Bright Light and the Rising Sun
I call to you Spirit in Gratitude for this day
I call to you Spirit and I ask you for your aid
Spirit of the East, may I begin with joy in my heart
May I access your far-reaching insight
May I rise above my problems
For an overview, with you.
Blessings on you, Spirit of the East. With love.

notes:

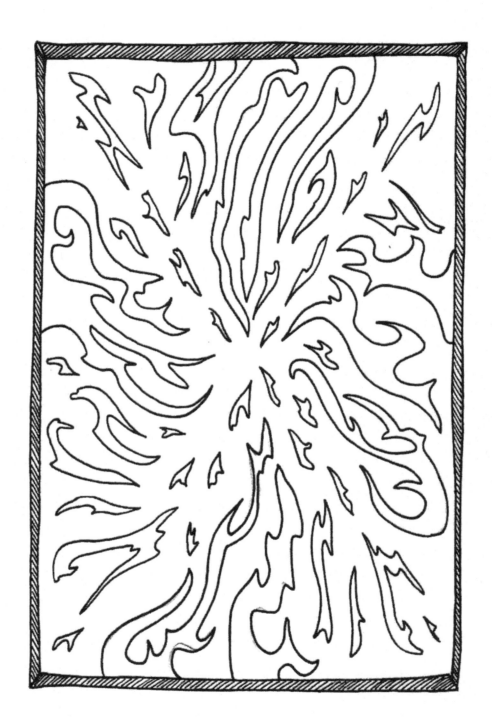

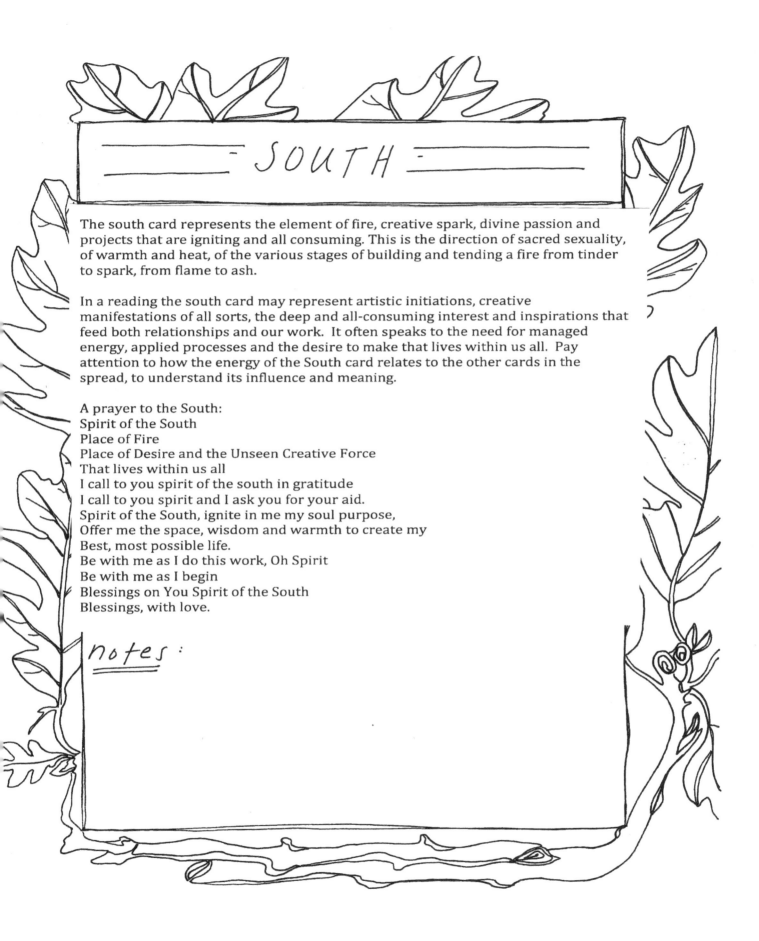

SOUTH

The south card represents the element of fire, creative spark, divine passion and projects that are igniting and all consuming. This is the direction of sacred sexuality, of warmth and heat, of the various stages of building and tending a fire from tinder to spark, from flame to ash.

In a reading the south card may represent artistic initiations, creative manifestations of all sorts, the deep and all-consuming interest and inspirations that feed both relationships and our work. It often speaks to the need for managed energy, applied processes and the desire to make that lives within us all. Pay attention to how the energy of the South card relates to the other cards in the spread, to understand its influence and meaning.

A prayer to the South:
Spirit of the South
Place of Fire
Place of Desire and the Unseen Creative Force
That lives within us all
I call to you spirit of the south in gratitude
I call to you spirit and I ask you for your aid.
Spirit of the South, ignite in me my soul purpose,
Offer me the space, wisdom and warmth to create my
Best, most possible life.
Be with me as I do this work, Oh Spirit
Be with me as I begin
Blessings on You Spirit of the South
Blessings, with love.

notes:

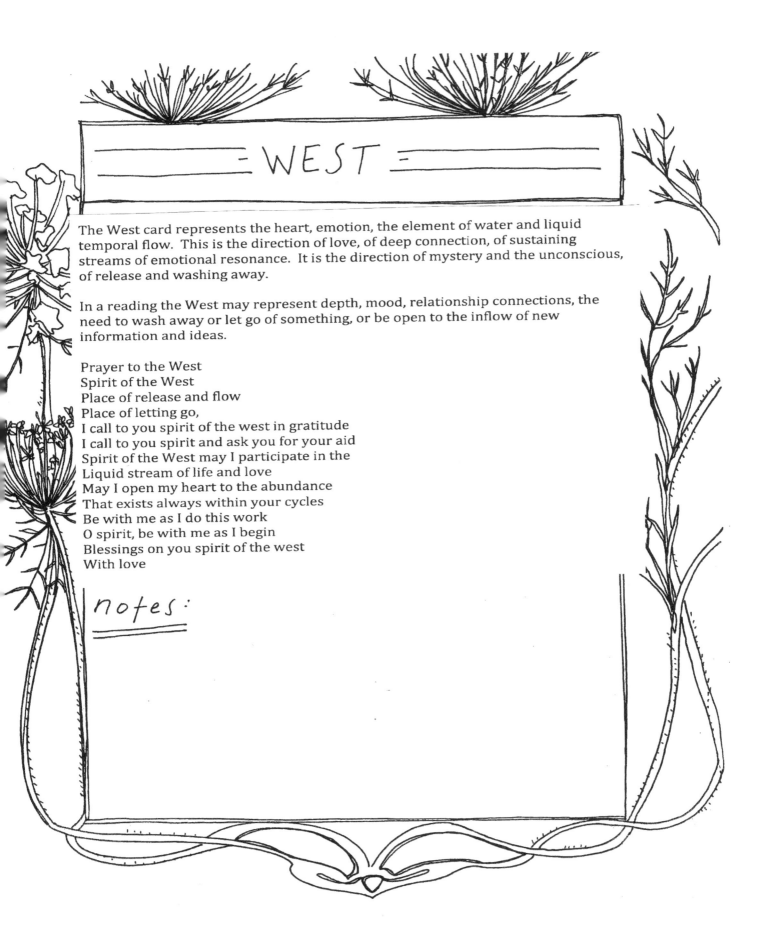

WEST

The West card represents the heart, emotion, the element of water and liquid temporal flow. This is the direction of love, of deep connection, of sustaining streams of emotional resonance. It is the direction of mystery and the unconscious, of release and washing away.

In a reading the West may represent depth, mood, relationship connections, the need to wash away or let go of something, or be open to the inflow of new information and ideas.

Prayer to the West
Spirit of the West
Place of release and flow
Place of letting go,
I call to you spirit of the west in gratitude
I call to you spirit and ask you for your aid
Spirit of the West may I participate in the
Liquid stream of life and love
May I open my heart to the abundance
That exists always within your cycles
Be with me as I do this work
O spirit, be with me as I begin
Blessings on you spirit of the west
With love

notes:

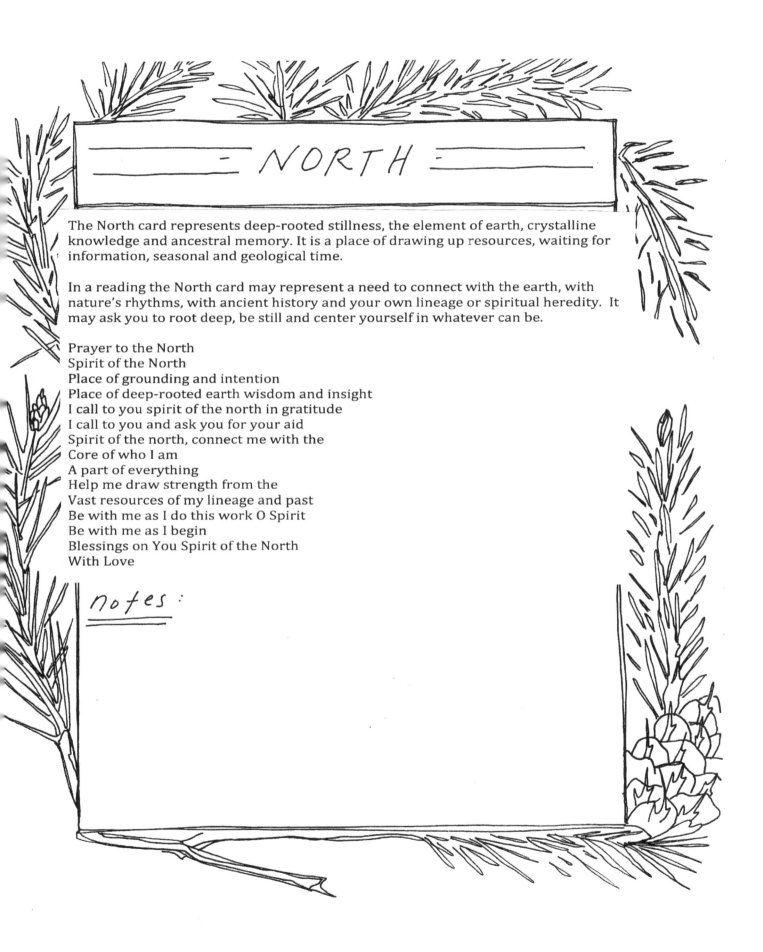

= NORTH =

The North card represents deep-rooted stillness, the element of earth, crystalline knowledge and ancestral memory. It is a place of drawing up resources, waiting for information, seasonal and geological time.

In a reading the North card may represent a need to connect with the earth, with nature's rhythms, with ancient history and your own lineage or spiritual heredity. It may ask you to root deep, be still and center yourself in whatever can be.

Prayer to the North
Spirit of the North
Place of grounding and intention
Place of deep-rooted earth wisdom and insight
I call to you spirit of the north in gratitude
I call to you and ask you for your aid
Spirit of the north, connect me with the
Core of who I am
A part of everything
Help me draw strength from the
Vast resources of my lineage and past
Be with me as I do this work O Spirit
Be with me as I begin
Blessings on You Spirit of the North
With Love

notes:

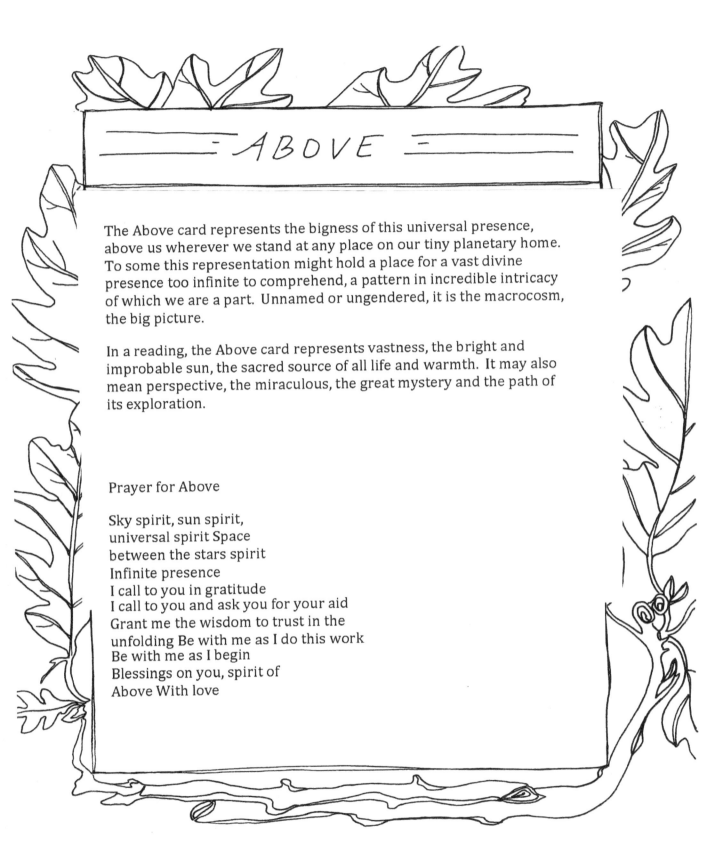

ABOVE

The Above card represents the bigness of this universal presence, above us wherever we stand at any place on our tiny planetary home. To some this representation might hold a place for a vast divine presence too infinite to comprehend, a pattern in incredible intricacy of which we are a part. Unnamed or ungendered, it is the macrocosm, the big picture.

In a reading, the Above card represents vastness, the bright and improbable sun, the sacred source of all life and warmth. It may also mean perspective, the miraculous, the great mystery and the path of its exploration.

Prayer for Above

Sky spirit, sun spirit,
universal spirit Space
between the stars spirit
Infinite presence
I call to you in gratitude
I call to you and ask you for your aid
Grant me the wisdom to trust in the
unfolding Be with me as I do this work
Be with me as I begin
Blessings on you, spirit of
Above With love

BELOW

The Below card represents the wisdom of the sacred earth, the living creative world, cycles of birth and death, emergence, rot and regeneration. Below is the microcosm, intricate life moving beneath us, all of the miniscule systems on which we depend but rarely see, the inverse of above, a sacred paradox. In a reading below represents natural rhythm, plant and animal cycles, interrelationship, wildness, wilderness, the delicate balance of living and dying. It may mean time in nature, a natural pause or movement through a transition, restoration of balance, attention to the details, gratitude and appreciation, or a need to establish a relationship with nature and the necessity of decomposition for growth.

Below Prayer

Sacred ancient,
Holy earth beneath me, sustainer of
life   I call to you in gratitude
I call to ancient cycle, beginning and
end,
Help me remember: I am of this
sacred earth
I am of this sacred life
Help me to feel the wisdom of this
heritage This lineage of earth and
place
The blessings of the cycle, birth and
death
Necessary rot, rebirth
Be with me as I do this
work
Be with me as I begin
Blessings on you spirit Below,
With love

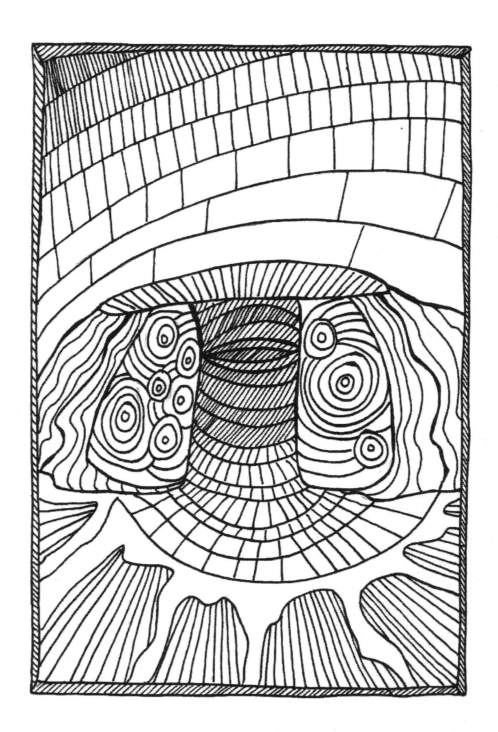

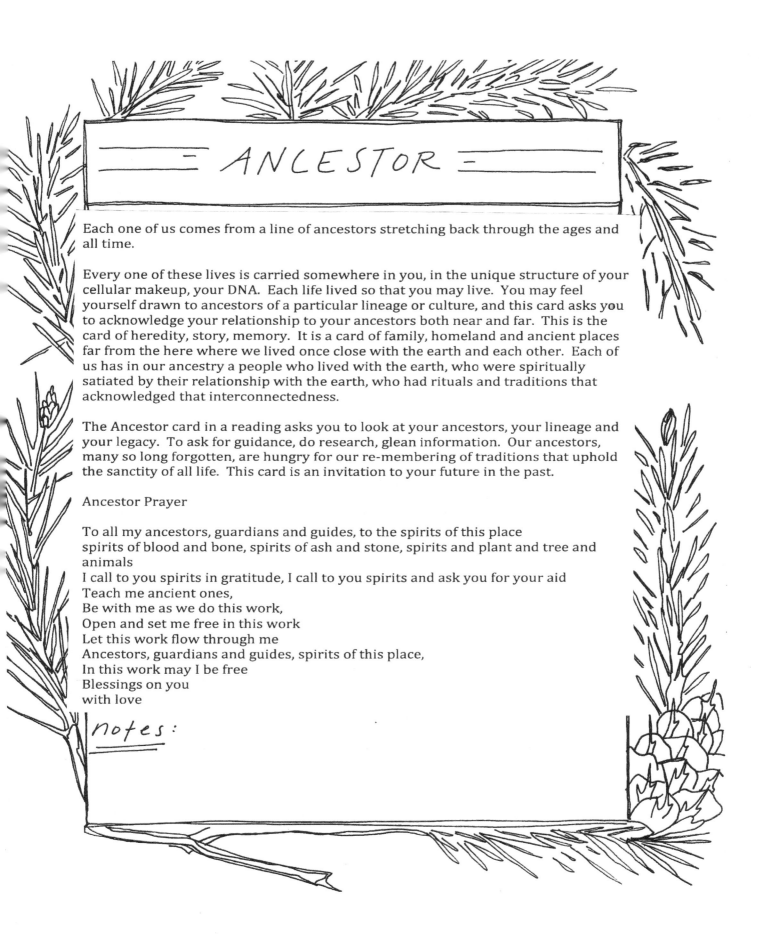

ANCESTOR

Each one of us comes from a line of ancestors stretching back through the ages and all time.

Every one of these lives is carried somewhere in you, in the unique structure of your cellular makeup, your DNA. Each life lived so that you may live. You may feel yourself drawn to ancestors of a particular lineage or culture, and this card asks you to acknowledge your relationship to your ancestors both near and far. This is the card of heredity, story, memory. It is a card of family, homeland and ancient places far from the here where we lived once close with the earth and each other. Each of us has in our ancestry a people who lived with the earth, who were spiritually satiated by their relationship with the earth, who had rituals and traditions that acknowledged that interconnectedness.

The Ancestor card in a reading asks you to look at your ancestors, your lineage and your legacy. To ask for guidance, do research, glean information. Our ancestors, many so long forgotten, are hungry for our re-membering of traditions that uphold the sanctity of all life. This card is an invitation to your future in the past.

Ancestor Prayer

To all my ancestors, guardians and guides, to the spirits of this place
spirits of blood and bone, spirits of ash and stone, spirits and plant and tree and animals
I call to you spirits in gratitude, I call to you spirits and ask you for your aid
Teach me ancient ones,
Be with me as we do this work,
Open and set me free in this work
Let this work flow through me
Ancestors, guardians and guides, spirits of this place,
In this work may I be free
Blessings on you
with love

notes:

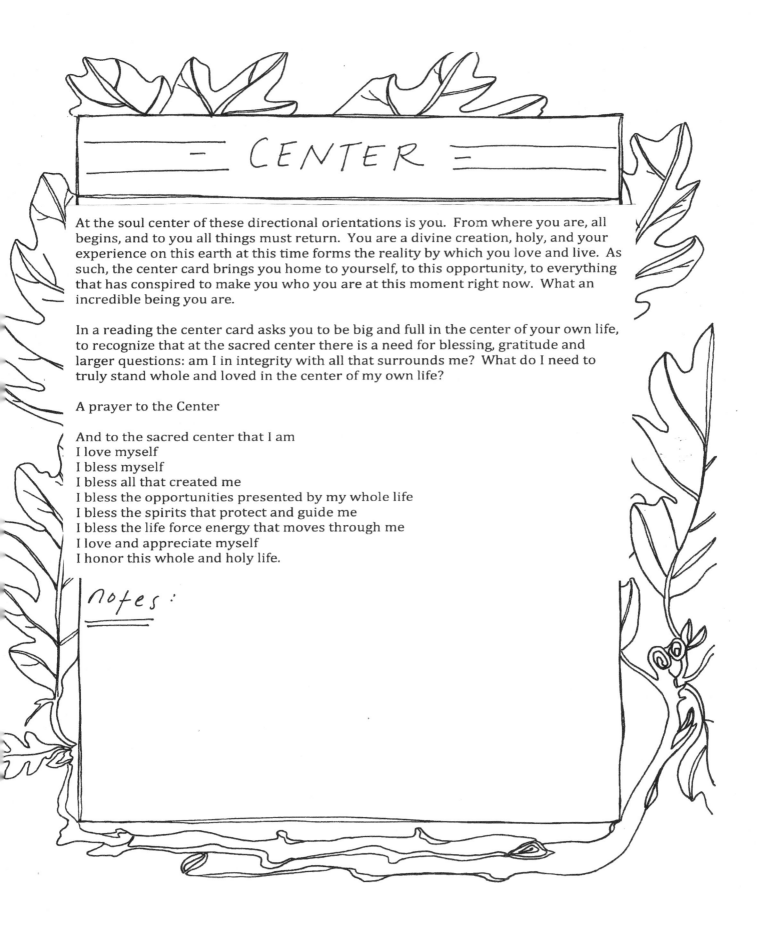

CENTER

At the soul center of these directional orientations is you. From where you are, all begins, and to you all things must return. You are a divine creation, holy, and your experience on this earth at this time forms the reality by which you love and live. As such, the center card brings you home to yourself, to this opportunity, to everything that has conspired to make you who you are at this moment right now. What an incredible being you are.

In a reading the center card asks you to be big and full in the center of your own life, to recognize that at the sacred center there is a need for blessing, gratitude and larger questions: am I in integrity with all that surrounds me? What do I need to truly stand whole and loved in the center of my own life?

A prayer to the Center

And to the sacred center that I am
I love myself
I bless myself
I bless all that created me
I bless the opportunities presented by my whole life
I bless the spirits that protect and guide me
I bless the life force energy that moves through me
I love and appreciate myself
I honor this whole and holy life.

notes:

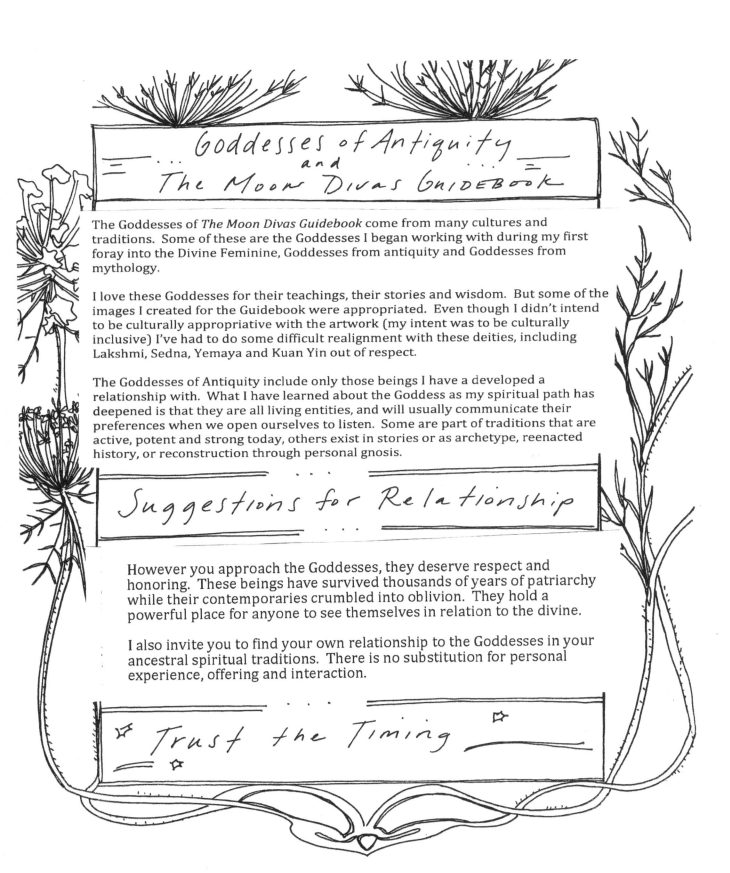

Goddesses of Antiquity and The Moon Divas Guidebook

The Goddesses of *The Moon Divas Guidebook* come from many cultures and traditions. Some of these are the Goddesses I began working with during my first foray into the Divine Feminine, Goddesses from antiquity and Goddesses from mythology.

I love these Goddesses for their teachings, their stories and wisdom. But some of the images I created for the Guidebook were appropriated. Even though I didn't intend to be culturally appropriative with the artwork (my intent was to be culturally inclusive) I've had to do some difficult realignment with these deities, including Lakshmi, Sedna, Yemaya and Kuan Yin out of respect.

The Goddesses of Antiquity include only those beings I have a developed a relationship with. What I have learned about the Goddess as my spiritual path has deepened is that they are all living entities, and will usually communicate their preferences when we open ourselves to listen. Some are part of traditions that are active, potent and strong today, others exist in stories or as archetype, reenacted history, or reconstruction through personal gnosis.

Suggestions for Relationship

However you approach the Goddesses, they deserve respect and honoring. These beings have survived thousands of years of patriarchy while their contemporaries crumbled into oblivion. They hold a powerful place for anyone to see themselves in relation to the divine.

I also invite you to find your own relationship to the Goddesses in your ancestral spiritual traditions. There is no substitution for personal experience, offering and interaction.

Trust the Timing

the Lady of Ephesus inspired by a statue ... from the 1st century ... C.E.

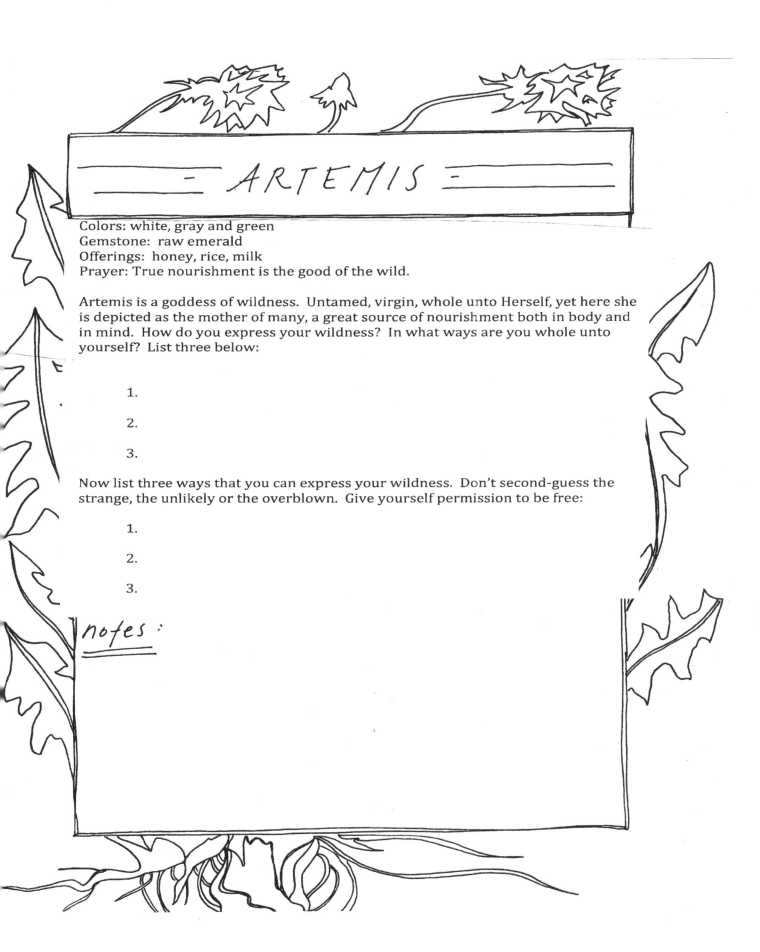

ARTEMIS

Colors: white, gray and green
Gemstone: raw emerald
Offerings: honey, rice, milk
Prayer: True nourishment is the good of the wild.

Artemis is a goddess of wildness. Untamed, virgin, whole unto Herself, yet here she is depicted as the mother of many, a great source of nourishment both in body and in mind. How do you express your wildness? In what ways are you whole unto yourself? List three below:

1.

2.

3.

Now list three ways that you can express your wildness. Don't second-guess the strange, the unlikely or the overblown. Give yourself permission to be free:

1.

2.

3.

notes:

Venus of Willendorf ~ Interpretation of Statue Crafted in ~22,000 = BCE

VENUS of WILLENDORF

Colors: many shades of stone
Gemstone: jasper
Offerings: roots, seeds, bark
Prayer: Time is time and change is change.

This Venus teaches the ancient wisdom of the body, a larger and more embedded truth than we usually encounter. In what ways do you connect with your body daily? Write some below...brushing your teeth or hair, taking a shower...

Take any one of these activities and imagine a way to ritualize it, to set it apart from the daily chores and make it truly meaningful. Maybe you could bless your hairbrush and brush your hair slowly and deliberately while you hum a song or say a positive intention for the day.

Honoring your body with mini rituals will make the larger tasks of self-care (like taking a day off to rest or getting a massage) feel more manageable. Rooting into the beauty of your larger physical being strengthens your intentions and helps them to manifest.

notes :

FREYJA

Gemstone: amber, the tears she cried
Offerings: distaff, spun wool, beautiful beads, wooden combs
Prayer: I am whole, fierce, beloved and free.

Freyja is an ancient Goddess. Her name means Lady, but she has many titles through all of the North as the Goddess of Love and Beauty, Mistress of Cats, Queen of the Valkyrie and Sacred Sow.

Freyja in ancient myth is a far greater presence than the typical contemporary sex symbol. While eroticism and embodiment are part of her power, she is also an ancestral matriarch, psychopomp ruler of the warrior dead in battle, sorceress and keeper of feminine specific magic. Reimagining her story brings us to a pre-patriarchal world, where women defied simple categorization. Freyja allows us to embrace contradiction and simultaneity, and refuse easy containment by those who underestimate our power.

Many of the stories about Freyja emphasize her autonomy. She makes choices on her own, faces truths some find unpleasant, and remains strong in the face of ridicule. She honors her own mind, regardless of what anyone thinks or says.

List five ways you can empower yourself each and every day, without exception.

1.

2.

3.

4.

5.

How can you find power in honoring your own truth?

THE MORRIGAN

Colors: rich spectrum of greens, grey of sky and sea, chalk white, blood red, black
Gemstone: calcite, fluorite, quartz
Offerings: earth from the barrow mound or cave mouth, flax or nettles, clean water
Prayer: Open, Open, Open, Receive, Receive, Receive

The Morrígan is an ancient Celtic Goddess with a multitude of aspects. Her name means Great Queen, and she represents the autonomous sovereignty of women and the sacred land. Here she guards the death chamber, the barrow mound, inviting entry and departure from the womb of the mother earth.

In this culture death is often avoided, seen as negative or frightening. The Morrígan reminds us that death is every ending, every turning of the wheel, a necessary clearing, an opening and transformation.

Where are you called to investigate death, literally or metaphorically, in your life?

What phase of transition are you entering, occupying or emerging from? Do you stand outside the tomb, rest within it, or are you preparing for rebirth? Spend some time exploring the beauty of death as a cycle that supports us in new ways of living.

notes:

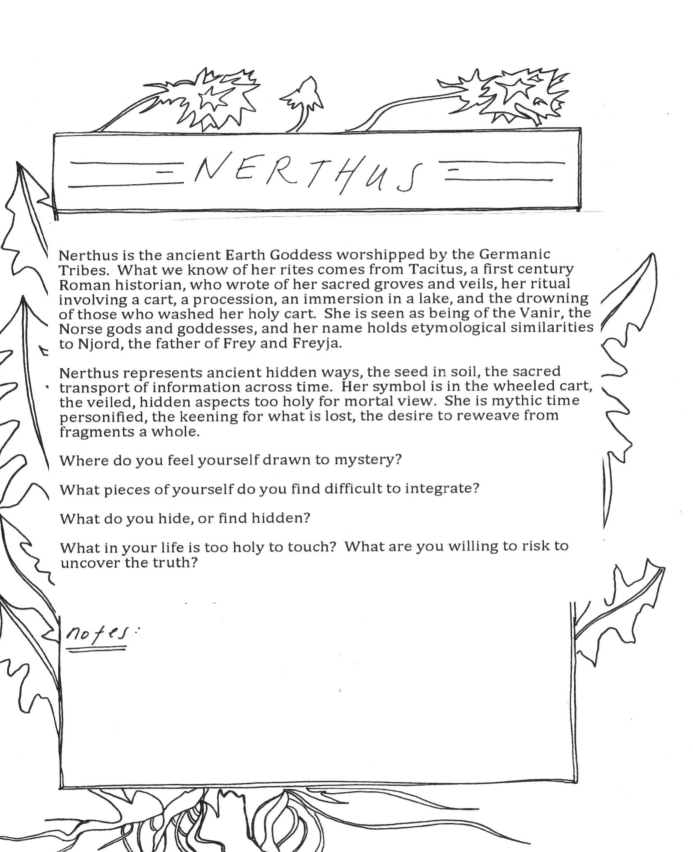

NERTHUS

Nerthus is the ancient Earth Goddess worshipped by the Germanic Tribes. What we know of her rites comes from Tacitus, a first century Roman historian, who wrote of her sacred groves and veils, her ritual involving a cart, a procession, an immersion in a lake, and the drowning of those who washed her holy cart. She is seen as being of the Vanir, the Norse gods and goddesses, and her name holds etymological similarities to Njord, the father of Frey and Freyja.

Nerthus represents ancient hidden ways, the seed in soil, the sacred transport of information across time. Her symbol is in the wheeled cart, the veiled, hidden aspects too holy for mortal view. She is mythic time personified, the keening for what is lost, the desire to reweave from fragments a whole.

Where do you feel yourself drawn to mystery?

What pieces of yourself do you find difficult to integrate?

What do you hide, or find hidden?

What in your life is too holy to touch? What are you willing to risk to uncover the truth?

notes:

Sunna-Sól, Lan Vesta '16

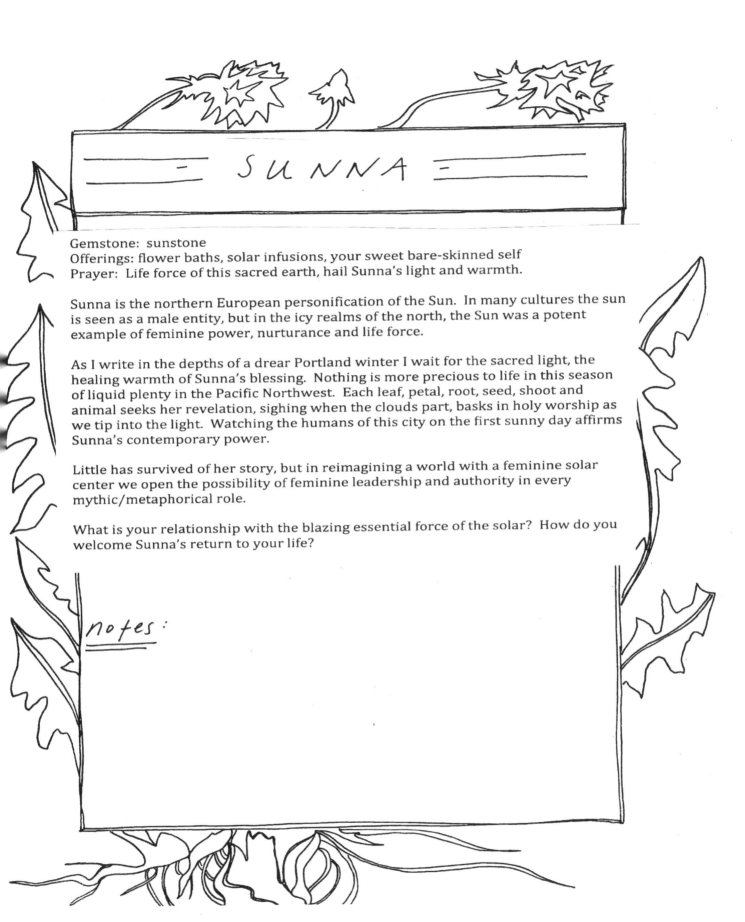

SUNNA

Gemstone: sunstone
Offerings: flower baths, solar infusions, your sweet bare-skinned self
Prayer: Life force of this sacred earth, hail Sunna's light and warmth.

Sunna is the northern European personification of the Sun. In many cultures the sun is seen as a male entity, but in the icy realms of the north, the Sun was a potent example of feminine power, nurturance and life force.

As I write in the depths of a drear Portland winter I wait for the sacred light, the healing warmth of Sunna's blessing. Nothing is more precious to life in this season of liquid plenty in the Pacific Northwest. Each leaf, petal, root, seed, shoot and animal seeks her revelation, sighing when the clouds part, basks in holy worship as we tip into the light. Watching the humans of this city on the first sunny day affirms Sunna's contemporary power.

Little has survived of her story, but in reimagining a world with a feminine solar center we open the possibility of feminine leadership and authority in every mythic/metaphorical role.

What is your relationship with the blazing essential force of the solar? How do you welcome Sunna's return to your life?

notes:

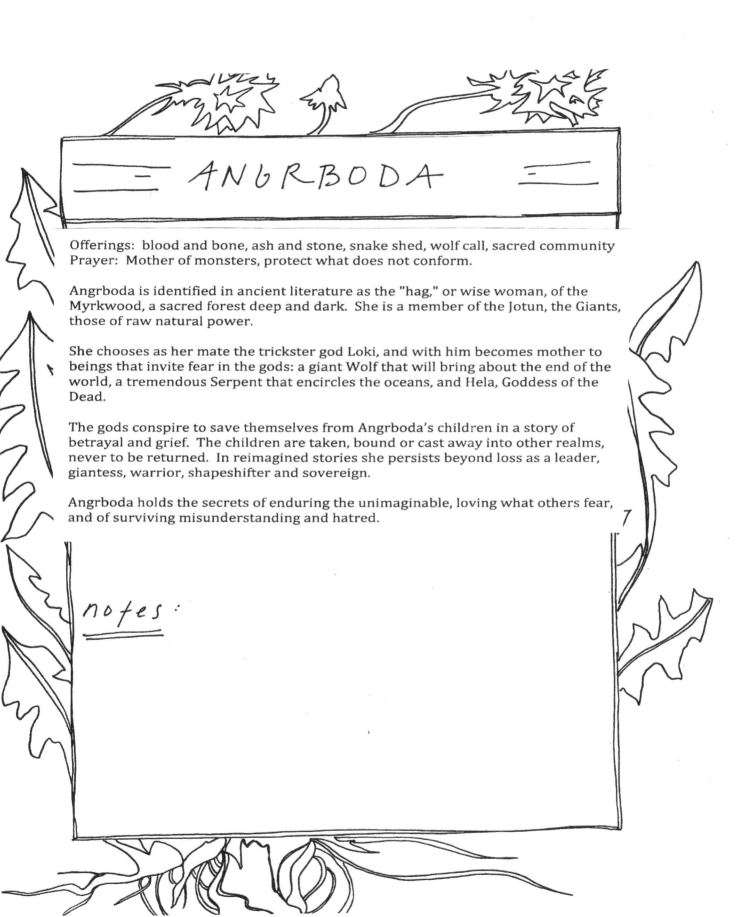

ANGRBODA

Offerings: blood and bone, ash and stone, snake shed, wolf call, sacred community
Prayer: Mother of monsters, protect what does not conform.

Angrboda is identified in ancient literature as the "hag," or wise woman, of the Myrkwood, a sacred forest deep and dark. She is a member of the Jotun, the Giants, those of raw natural power.

She chooses as her mate the trickster god Loki, and with him becomes mother to beings that invite fear in the gods: a giant Wolf that will bring about the end of the world, a tremendous Serpent that encircles the oceans, and Hela, Goddess of the Dead.

The gods conspire to save themselves from Angrboda's children in a story of betrayal and grief. The children are taken, bound or cast away into other realms, never to be returned. In reimagined stories she persists beyond loss as a leader, giantess, warrior, shapeshifter and sovereign.

Angrboda holds the secrets of enduring the unimaginable, loving what others fear, and of surviving misunderstanding and hatred.

notes:

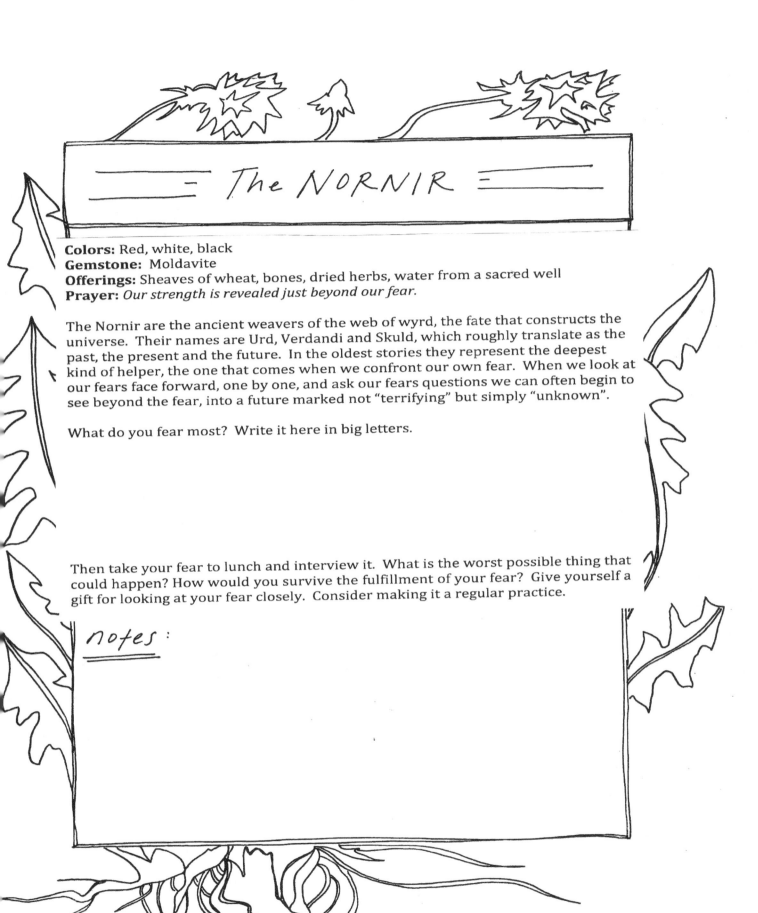

The NORNIR

Colors: Red, white, black
Gemstone: Moldavite
Offerings: Sheaves of wheat, bones, dried herbs, water from a sacred well
Prayer: *Our strength is revealed just beyond our fear.*

The Nornir are the ancient weavers of the web of wyrd, the fate that constructs the universe. Their names are Urd, Verdandi and Skuld, which roughly translate as the past, the present and the future. In the oldest stories they represent the deepest kind of helper, the one that comes when we confront our own fear. When we look at our fears face forward, one by one, and ask our fears questions we can often begin to see beyond the fear, into a future marked not "terrifying" but simply "unknown".

What do you fear most? Write it here in big letters.

Then take your fear to lunch and interview it. What is the worst possible thing that could happen? How would you survive the fulfillment of your fear? Give yourself a gift for looking at your fear closely. Consider making it a regular practice.

notes:

10·31·15

HELA

Colors: Grey, blue, black
Gemstone: Petrified wood, onyx, obsidian
Offerings: Blood and bone, ash and stone
Prayer: *In every ending, a beginning. In every death, rebirth.*

Hela is the child of the Giantess Angrboda and the God Loki. She was born half living and half dead, so she knows a thing or two about being different, ostracized and lonely. When she was still a child, Hela was taken from her parents and thrown into Helheim, the land of the dead, by Gods who were afraid of her power.

Here she made a home for herself, as a Goddess and ruler, tender of the sacred dead.

Where have you felt different, like an outcast, or that you don't fit in or belong? Do you have passions or interests that you feel require an apology? Is there a confrontation you have been avoiding? In the space below, illustrate your conflict or reticence.

In the coming week, be mindful of the places you are apologizing for or avoiding. Keep one apology to yourself, or engage in a tough conversation. Give yourself permission to be bold, embrace your difference and rule from a place of power in your own life.

GULLVEIG - HEID

Colors: Liquid gold.
Gemstones: Rutilated quartz,
Offering: Sacred fire.
Prayer: *You cannot kill what will not die.*

In the Norse myths, Gullveig is the Goddess whose abuse begins the first war in the world. Her name means gold drink, and there are many interpretations as to her origin and significance. Gullveig is kidnapped by Gods outside her clan. They stab her with spears and burn her three times.

But each time she is reborn.

After the third burning, Gullveig emerges with a new name, as the Goddess Heid, which means shining. From her initiation she retrieves a gift, a specific form of magic known as seidr, which she practices from then on openly and without fear.

Where in your life have you experienced painful initiation? We speak metaphorically of being "burned" by others, betrayed or harmed. What gifts have you found in these experiences?

Gullveig/Heid teaches us how to survive the unthinkable and emerge powerfully from the ashes, to begin anew. What new name could you assume to define your stronger state of being?

notes:

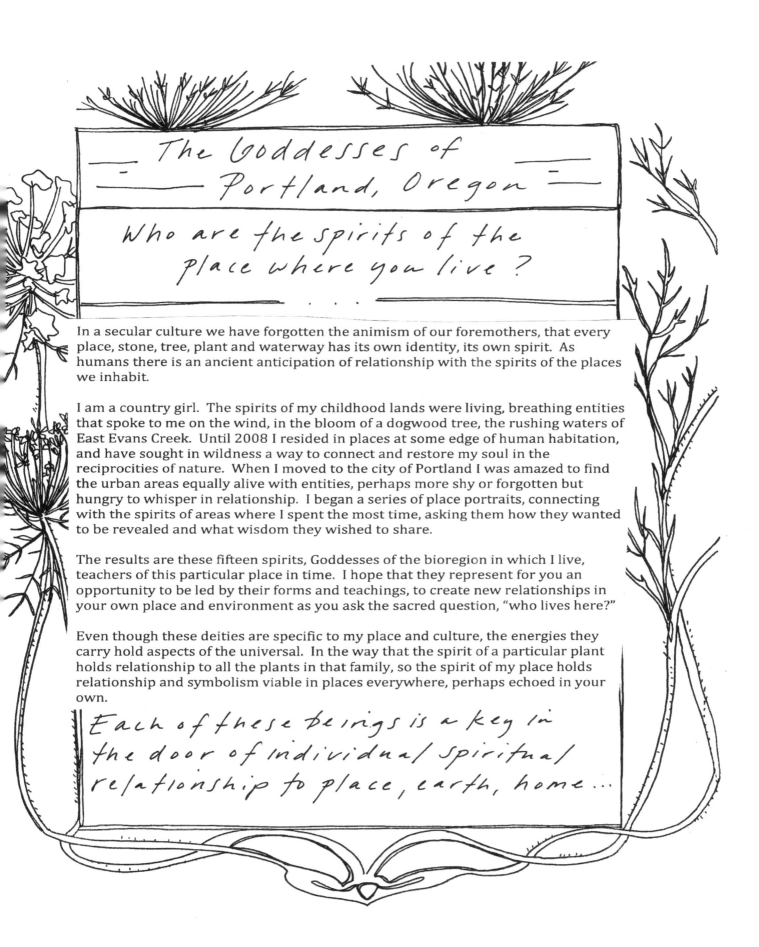

The Goddesses of Portland, Oregon

Who are the spirits of the place where you live?

In a secular culture we have forgotten the animism of our foremothers, that every place, stone, tree, plant and waterway has its own identity, its own spirit. As humans there is an ancient anticipation of relationship with the spirits of the places we inhabit.

I am a country girl. The spirits of my childhood lands were living, breathing entities that spoke to me on the wind, in the bloom of a dogwood tree, the rushing waters of East Evans Creek. Until 2008 I resided in places at some edge of human habitation, and have sought in wildness a way to connect and restore my soul in the reciprocities of nature. When I moved to the city of Portland I was amazed to find the urban areas equally alive with entities, perhaps more shy or forgotten but hungry to whisper in relationship. I began a series of place portraits, connecting with the spirits of areas where I spent the most time, asking them how they wanted to be revealed and what wisdom they wished to share.

The results are these fifteen spirits, Goddesses of the bioregion in which I live, teachers of this particular place in time. I hope that they represent for you an opportunity to be led by their forms and teachings, to create new relationships in your own place and environment as you ask the sacred question, "who lives here?"

Even though these deities are specific to my place and culture, the energies they carry hold aspects of the universal. In the way that the spirit of a particular plant holds relationship to all the plants in that family, so the spirit of my place holds relationship and symbolism viable in places everywhere, perhaps echoed in your own.

Each of these beings is a key in the door of individual spiritual relationship to place, earth, home…

water meet, such as off the shores of Elk Rock Island.

She is generous but demands a willingness to explore the depths.

FISKE is the goddess of passage and good boundaries. A shapeshifter, she is often spotted where stone and

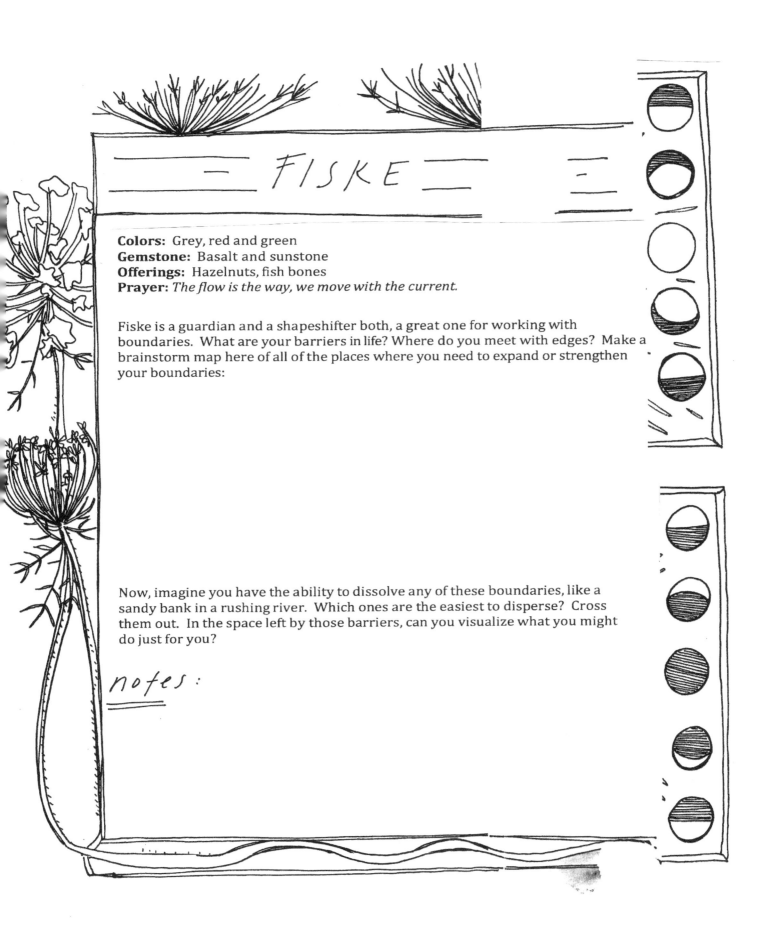

FISKE

Colors: Grey, red and green
Gemstone: Basalt and sunstone
Offerings: Hazelnuts, fish bones
Prayer: *The flow is the way, we move with the current.*

Fiske is a guardian and a shapeshifter both, a great one for working with boundaries. What are your barriers in life? Where do you meet with edges? Make a brainstorm map here of all of the places where you need to expand or strengthen your boundaries:

Now, imagine you have the ability to dissolve any of these boundaries, like a sandy bank in a rushing river. Which ones are the easiest to disperse? Cross them out. In the space left by those barriers, can you visualize what you might do just for you?

notes:

a mantle of   rain that feeds the

PORTLANDIA, patron goddess of Portland, Oregon. She wears

sacred rivers, Columbia and Willamette. Protector of waterways,

urban wildlife, pedestrians and cyclists, all trees.

80

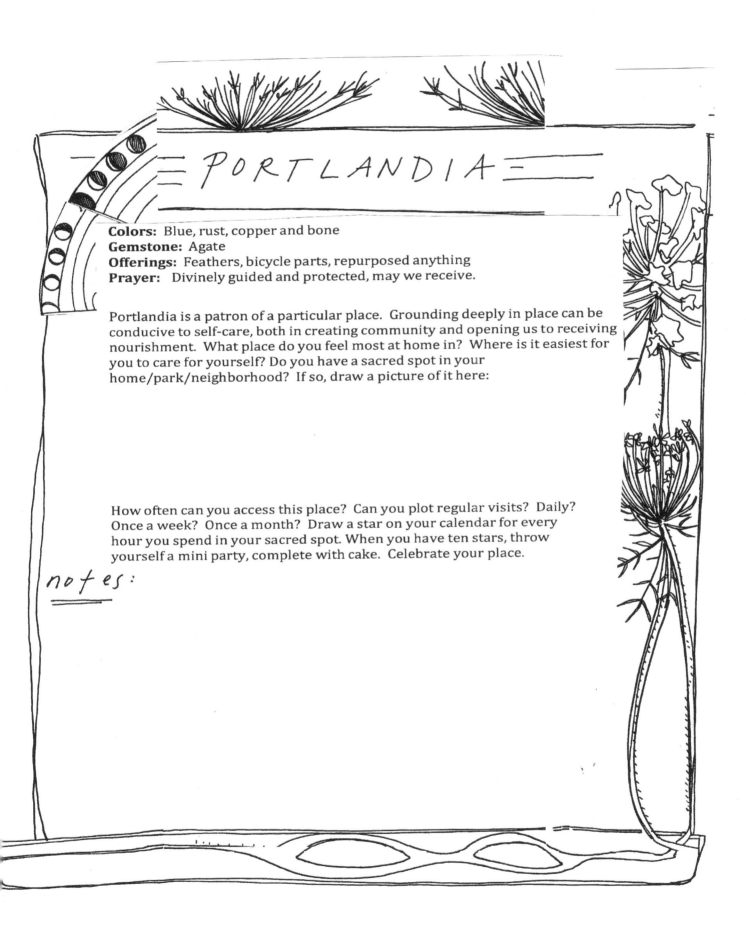

= PORTLANDIA =

Colors: Blue, rust, copper and bone
Gemstone: Agate
Offerings: Feathers, bicycle parts, repurposed anything
Prayer: Divinely guided and protected, may we receive.

Portlandia is a patron of a particular place. Grounding deeply in place can be conducive to self-care, both in creating community and opening us to receiving nourishment. What place do you feel most at home in? Where is it easiest for you to care for yourself? Do you have a sacred spot in your home/park/neighborhood? If so, draw a picture of it here:

How often can you access this place? Can you plot regular visits? Daily? Once a week? Once a month? Draw a star on your calendar for every hour you spend in your sacred spot. When you have ten stars, throw yourself a mini party, complete with cake. Celebrate your place.

notes:

portrayed as a chicken, represented by her feathered cap...

fertility, solar energy and subsistence gardens. She is most often

TERRA MERIDIANUS is the SE goddess of

= TERRA =

Colors: warm brights, earth tones
Gemstone: emerald and gold
Offerings: fresh bread, eggs or garden produce
Prayer: All is well in this moment, and so may it ever be.

Terra asks us to consider connection with the earth, its seasons, creatures and abundance in our self-care and daily living. A key component of successful self-care is making mindful mini-rituals of what we already do. How many ways can you connect with the earth in daily practice, using things that are a natural part of your life? List twenty ways here:

What about trying one of these out right now?

Add a practice to each day on your calendar. Keep it small and sweet, see where it takes you.

CREATIVITY

INSPIRATION

...MAMA DEA makes her home in the ancient Grandmother's Tree on Mt. Tabor. She teaches time-wisdom, weed medicine, wild nourishment and how to sustain the inner fire...

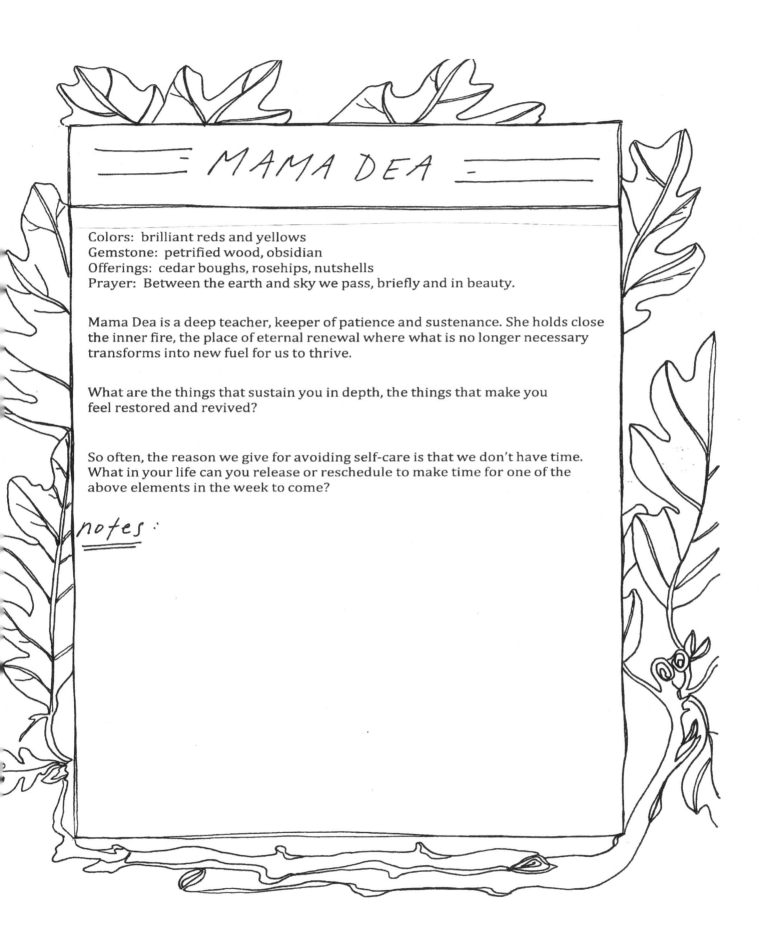

MAMA DEA

Colors: brilliant reds and yellows
Gemstone: petrified wood, obsidian
Offerings: cedar boughs, rosehips, nutshells
Prayer: Between the earth and sky we pass, briefly and in beauty.

Mama Dea is a deep teacher, keeper of patience and sustenance. She holds close the inner fire, the place of eternal renewal where what is no longer necessary transforms into new fuel for us to thrive.

What are the things that sustain you in depth, the things that make you feel restored and revived?

So often, the reason we give for avoiding self-care is that we don't have time. What in your life can you release or reschedule to make time for one of the above elements in the week to come?

notes:

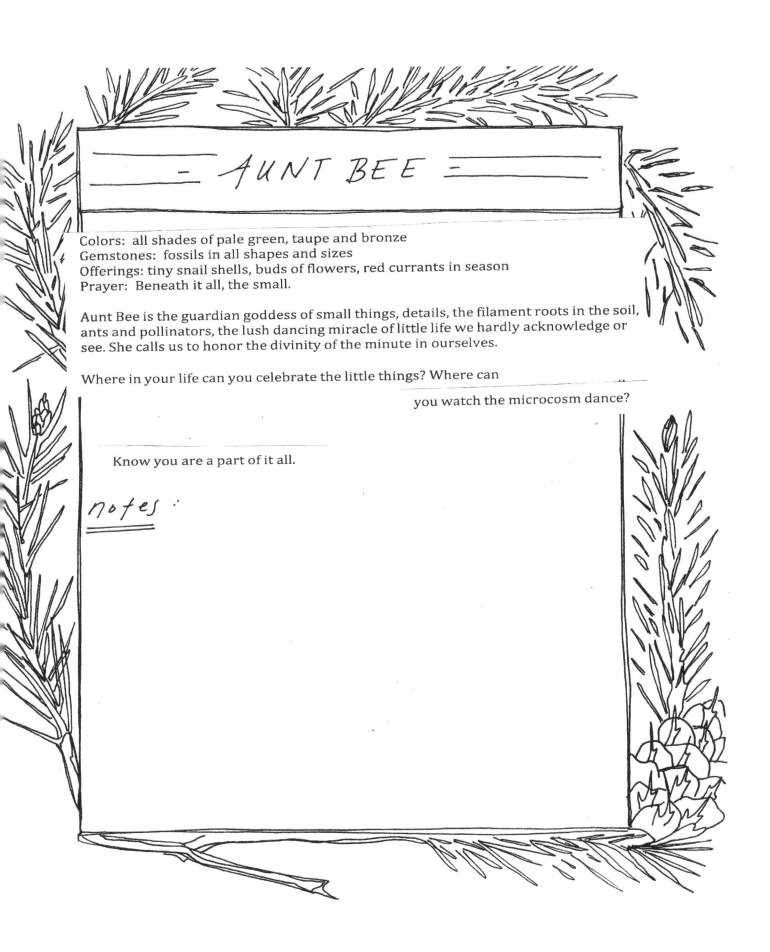

— AUNT BEE —

Colors: all shades of pale green, taupe and bronze
Gemstones: fossils in all shapes and sizes
Offerings: tiny snail shells, buds of flowers, red currants in season
Prayer: Beneath it all, the small.

Aunt Bee is the guardian goddess of small things, details, the filament roots in the soil, ants and pollinators, the lush dancing miracle of little life we hardly acknowledge or see. She calls us to honor the divinity of the minute in ourselves.

Where in your life can you celebrate the little things? Where can you watch the microcosm dance?

Know you are a part of it all.

notes :

LEDDY NIGHT carries within our ancestral

fear, as a place of rest.

is the bird of dreams, urging us to see the shadow sons

For city dwellers she memories of wildness, dark skies and stars.

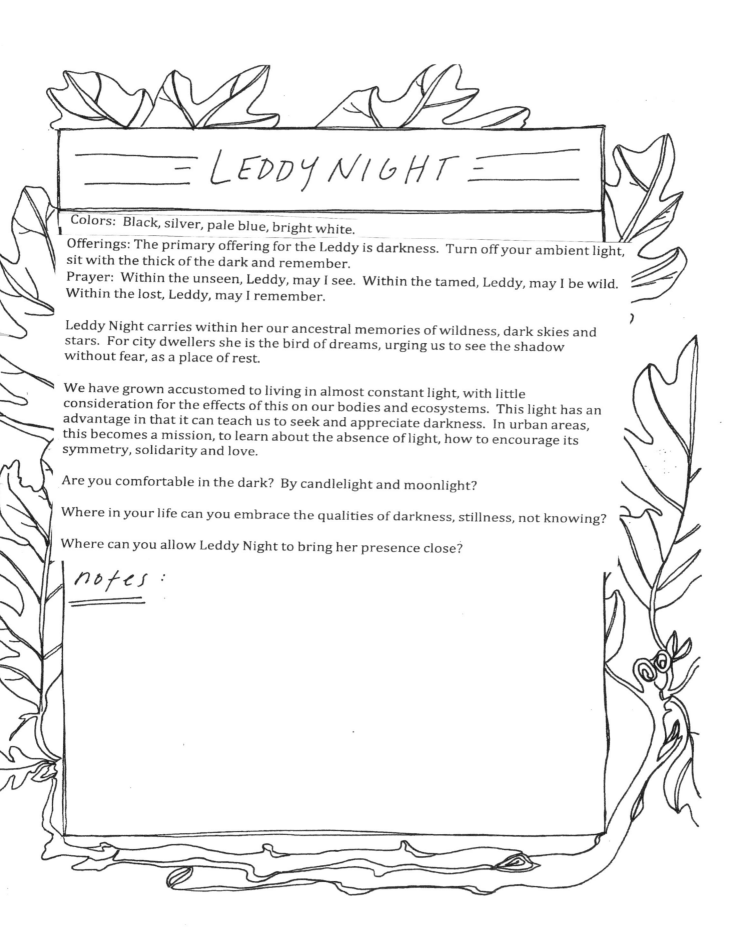

= LEDDY NIGHT =

Colors: Black, silver, pale blue, bright white.

Offerings: The primary offering for the Leddy is darkness. Turn off your ambient light, sit with the thick of the dark and remember.

Prayer: Within the unseen, Leddy, may I see. Within the tamed, Leddy, may I be wild. Within the lost, Leddy, may I remember.

Leddy Night carries within her our ancestral memories of wildness, dark skies and stars. For city dwellers she is the bird of dreams, urging us to see the shadow without fear, as a place of rest.

We have grown accustomed to living in almost constant light, with little consideration for the effects of this on our bodies and ecosystems. This light has an advantage in that it can teach us to seek and appreciate darkness. In urban areas, this becomes a mission, to learn about the absence of light, how to encourage its symmetry, solidarity and love.

Are you comfortable in the dark? By candlelight and moonlight?

Where in your life can you embrace the qualities of darkness, stillness, not knowing?

Where can you allow Leddy Night to bring her presence close?

notes:

..URDDA the RED ..

Rectifier. Keeper of justice for nature and women.

Her sweet face belies her fierceness. Beware.

= URDDA the RED =

Colors: All shades of red, rust and blood.
Jasper, bloodstone, clay.
Offerings: Menstrual blood on the earth, the sheddings of hair or fingernails. Pieces of yourself.
Prayer: May the balance be regained.

Urdda is a rectifier, the keeper of justice for nature and women whose lives are intricately intertwined. Her sweet face belies a fierceness. Beware her wrath.

Urdda may represent an area in your life that is out of balance, a place where an injustice has occurred or where a truth must be told. Is there a place where you need protection in your life and work? Is there an area where you need to speak your truth?

If someone has wronged you, Urdda encourages you to give your suffering to the earth. She will take it up and transform it into something fertile and new, if you trust her, if you allow.

Speaking Urdda's prayer when entering or leaving sacred space is a way to let the nature spirits know you value their place.

notes:

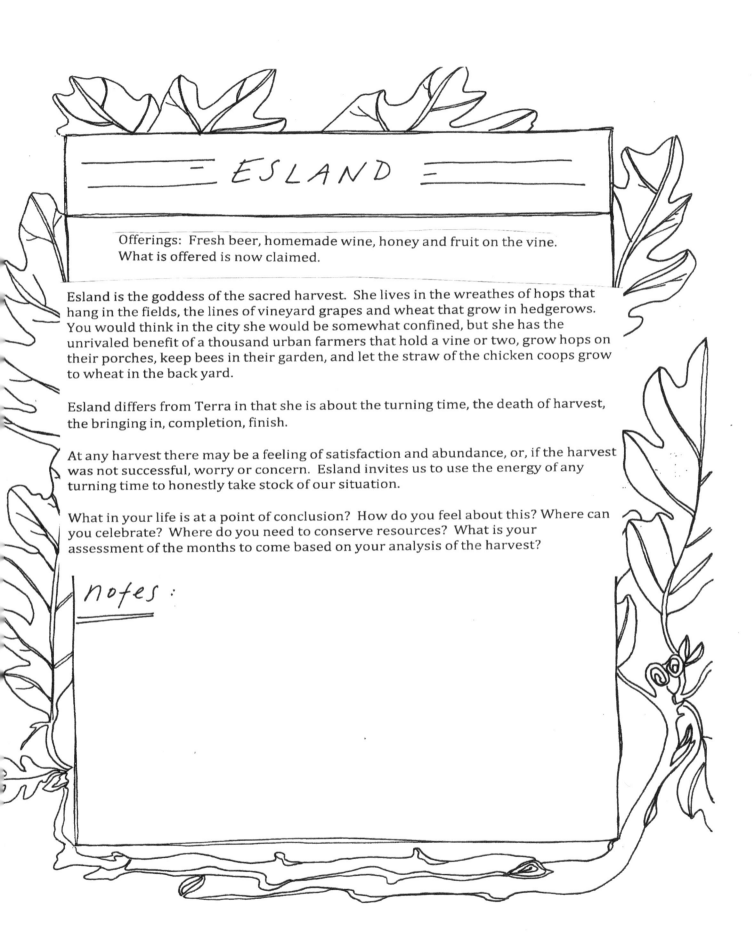

= ESLAND =

Offerings: Fresh beer, homemade wine, honey and fruit on the vine.
What is offered is now claimed.

Esland is the goddess of the sacred harvest. She lives in the wreathes of hops that hang in the fields, the lines of vineyard grapes and wheat that grow in hedgerows. You would think in the city she would be somewhat confined, but she has the unrivaled benefit of a thousand urban farmers that hold a vine or two, grow hops on their porches, keep bees in their garden, and let the straw of the chicken coops grow to wheat in the back yard.

Esland differs from Terra in that she is about the turning time, the death of harvest, the bringing in, completion, finish.

At any harvest there may be a feeling of satisfaction and abundance, or, if the harvest was not successful, worry or concern. Esland invites us to use the energy of any turning time to honestly take stock of our situation.

What in your life is at a point of conclusion? How do you feel about this? Where can you celebrate? Where do you need to conserve resources? What is your assessment of the months to come based on your analysis of the harvest?

notes:

GODDESS of CONFLUENCE

Colors: Deep blue, emerald green, indigo, slate grey.
Gemstones: Granite, jasper, sandstone,
Offerings: Any mixture of substances, like flower petals and water, essences and elixirs.
Prayer: Into one, the other, into the other, one.

Lelu is the Goddess of Confluence at the juncture of the Columbia and Willamette rivers. She is huge and roiling at her depths, carrying the deposits of thousands of miles of creeks and streams. She represents the joining of disparate forces, the need to mingle and merge in order to gain momentum and conserve energy.

Most modern people I know live their lives in many directions, assuming diverse roles. We keep some for our heart, some out of obligation. Lelu asks us to question the efficacy of not allowing flow in our lives. What are you giving your energy to out of obligation? Where would you like to merge forces, to place your heart? What would it take to consolidate your efforts in one direction? How can you begin, in small ways, droplet to rivulet to stream, to bring together what you truly love?

notes:

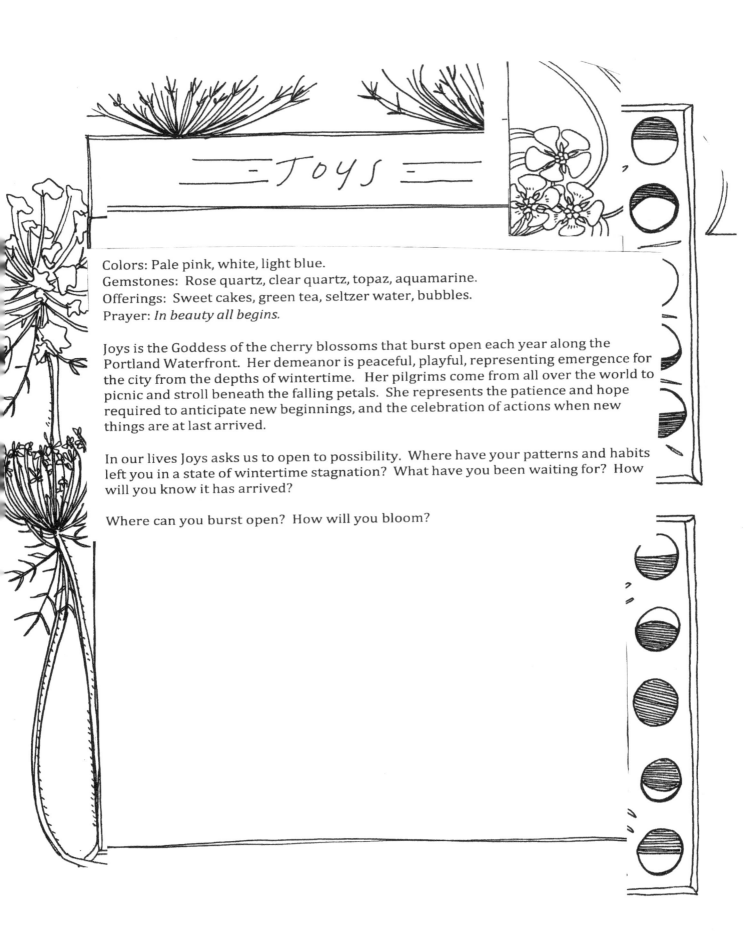

= JOYS =

Colors: Pale pink, white, light blue.
Gemstones: Rose quartz, clear quartz, topaz, aquamarine.
Offerings: Sweet cakes, green tea, seltzer water, bubbles.
Prayer: *In beauty all begins.*

Joys is the Goddess of the cherry blossoms that burst open each year along the Portland Waterfront. Her demeanor is peaceful, playful, representing emergence for the city from the depths of wintertime. Her pilgrims come from all over the world to picnic and stroll beneath the falling petals. She represents the patience and hope required to anticipate new beginnings, and the celebration of actions when new things are at last arrived.

In our lives Joys asks us to open to possibility. Where have your patterns and habits left you in a state of wintertime stagnation? What have you been waiting for? How will you know it has arrived?

Where can you burst open? How will you bloom?

GUARDIAN SPIRIT OF WAHKEENA FALLS BY MOONLIGHT

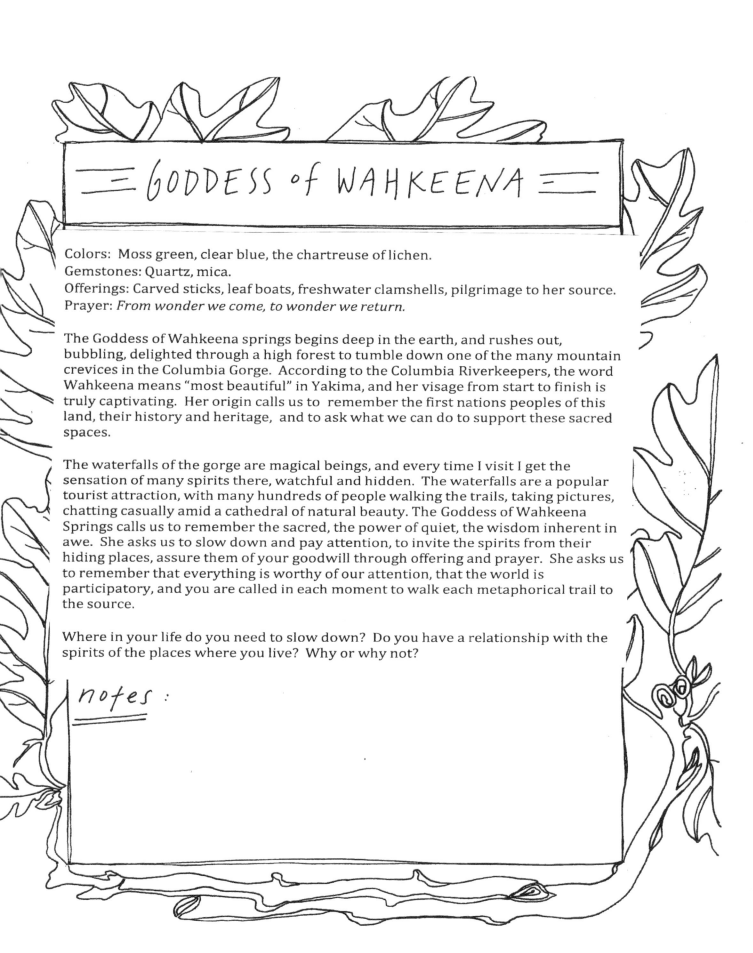

= GODDESS of WAHKEENA =

Colors: Moss green, clear blue, the chartreuse of lichen.
Gemstones: Quartz, mica.
Offerings: Carved sticks, leaf boats, freshwater clamshells, pilgrimage to her source.
Prayer: *From wonder we come, to wonder we return.*

The Goddess of Wahkeena springs begins deep in the earth, and rushes out, bubbling, delighted through a high forest to tumble down one of the many mountain crevices in the Columbia Gorge. According to the Columbia Riverkeepers, the word Wahkeena means "most beautiful" in Yakima, and her visage from start to finish is truly captivating. Her origin calls us to remember the first nations peoples of this land, their history and heritage, and to ask what we can do to support these sacred spaces.

The waterfalls of the gorge are magical beings, and every time I visit I get the sensation of many spirits there, watchful and hidden. The waterfalls are a popular tourist attraction, with many hundreds of people walking the trails, taking pictures, chatting casually amid a cathedral of natural beauty. The Goddess of Wahkeena Springs calls us to remember the sacred, the power of quiet, the wisdom inherent in awe. She asks us to slow down and pay attention, to invite the spirits from their hiding places, assure them of your goodwill through offering and prayer. She asks us to remember that everything is worthy of our attention, that the world is participatory, and you are called in each moment to walk each metaphorical trail to the source.

Where in your life do you need to slow down? Do you have a relationship with the spirits of the places where you live? Why or why not?

notes :

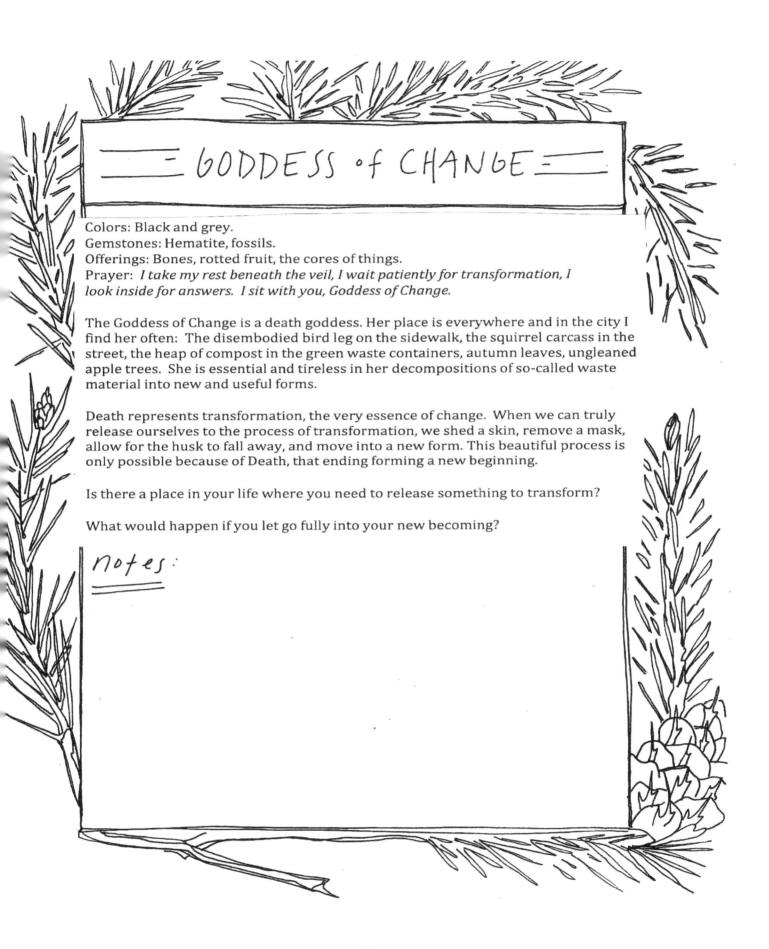

GODDESS of CHANGE

Colors: Black and grey.
Gemstones: Hematite, fossils.
Offerings: Bones, rotted fruit, the cores of things.
Prayer: *I take my rest beneath the veil, I wait patiently for transformation, I look inside for answers. I sit with you, Goddess of Change.*

The Goddess of Change is a death goddess. Her place is everywhere and in the city I find her often: The disembodied bird leg on the sidewalk, the squirrel carcass in the street, the heap of compost in the green waste containers, autumn leaves, ungleaned apple trees. She is essential and tireless in her decompositions of so-called waste material into new and useful forms.

Death represents transformation, the very essence of change. When we can truly release ourselves to the process of transformation, we shed a skin, remove a mask, allow for the husk to fall away, and move into a new form. This beautiful process is only possible because of Death, that ending forming a new beginning.

Is there a place in your life where you need to release something to transform?

What would happen if you let go fully into your new becoming?

notes:

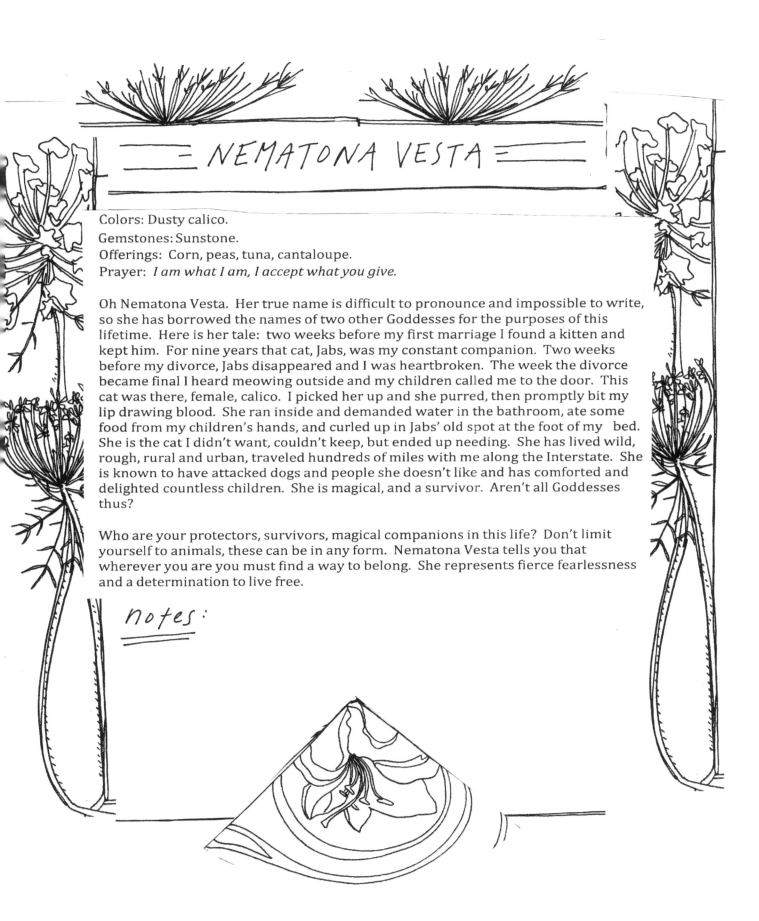

NEMATONA VESTA

Colors: Dusty calico.
Gemstones: Sunstone.
Offerings: Corn, peas, tuna, cantaloupe.
Prayer: *I am what I am, I accept what you give.*

Oh Nematona Vesta. Her true name is difficult to pronounce and impossible to write, so she has borrowed the names of two other Goddesses for the purposes of this lifetime. Here is her tale: two weeks before my first marriage I found a kitten and kept him. For nine years that cat, Jabs, was my constant companion. Two weeks before my divorce, Jabs disappeared and I was heartbroken. The week the divorce became final I heard meowing outside and my children called me to the door. This cat was there, female, calico. I picked her up and she purred, then promptly bit my lip drawing blood. She ran inside and demanded water in the bathroom, ate some food from my children's hands, and curled up in Jabs' old spot at the foot of my bed. She is the cat I didn't want, couldn't keep, but ended up needing. She has lived wild, rough, rural and urban, traveled hundreds of miles with me along the Interstate. She is known to have attacked dogs and people she doesn't like and has comforted and delighted countless children. She is magical, and a survivor. Aren't all Goddesses thus?

Who are your protectors, survivors, magical companions in this life? Don't limit yourself to animals, these can be in any form. Nematona Vesta tells you that wherever you are you must find a way to belong. She represents fierce fearlessness and a determination to live free.

notes:

Ver is the Goddess of sacred springs and forest pools. She is known for her gentleness as a protector and guardian of mothers and children. She holds the space for healing and hope within, carrying us all together.

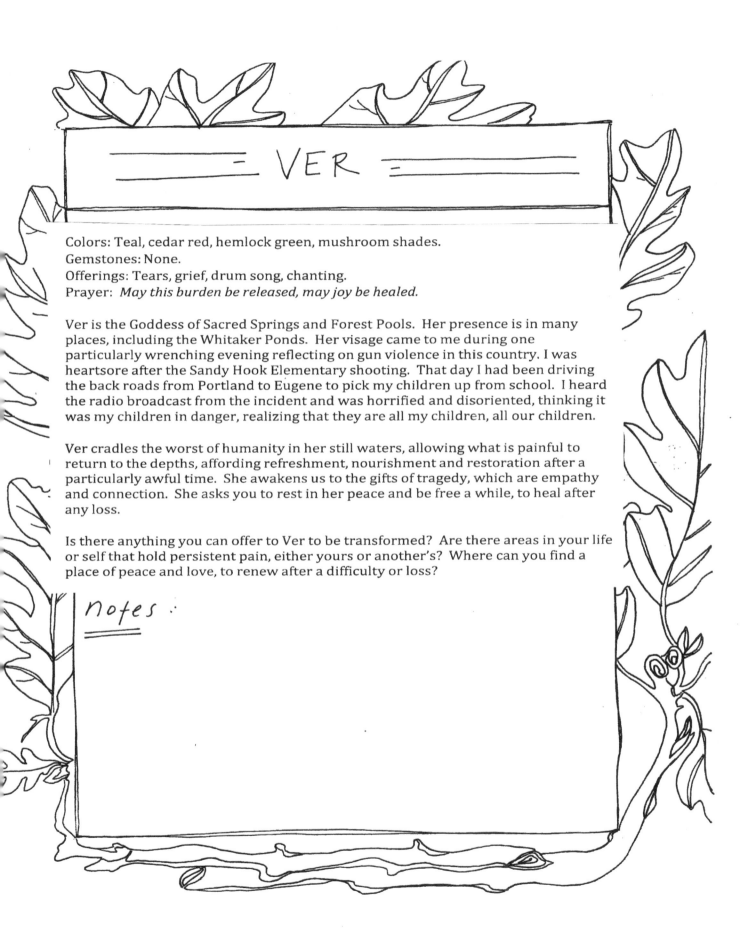

VER

Colors: Teal, cedar red, hemlock green, mushroom shades.
Gemstones: None.
Offerings: Tears, grief, drum song, chanting.
Prayer: *May this burden be released, may joy be healed.*

Ver is the Goddess of Sacred Springs and Forest Pools. Her presence is in many places, including the Whitaker Ponds. Her visage came to me during one particularly wrenching evening reflecting on gun violence in this country. I was heartsore after the Sandy Hook Elementary shooting. That day I had been driving the back roads from Portland to Eugene to pick my children up from school. I heard the radio broadcast from the incident and was horrified and disoriented, thinking it was my children in danger, realizing that they are all my children, all our children.

Ver cradles the worst of humanity in her still waters, allowing what is painful to return to the depths, affording refreshment, nourishment and restoration after a particularly awful time. She awakens us to the gifts of tragedy, which are empathy and connection. She asks you to rest in her peace and be free a while, to heal after any loss.

Is there anything you can offer to Ver to be transformed? Are there areas in your life or self that hold persistent pain, either yours or another's? Where can you find a place of peace and love, to renew after a difficulty or loss?

notes:

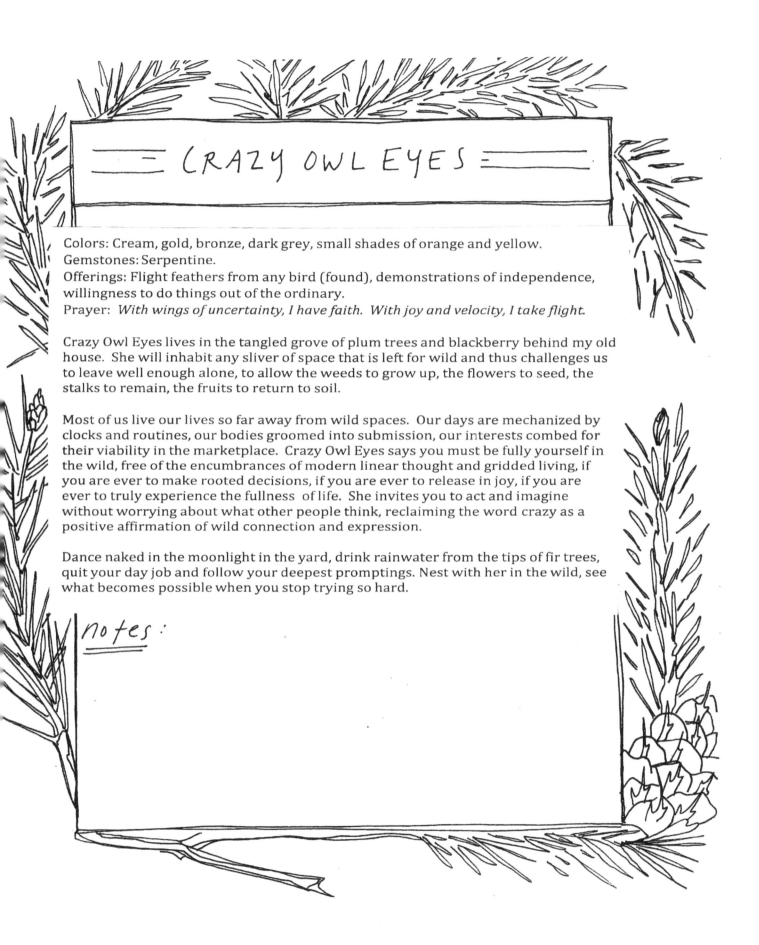

CRAZY OWL EYES

Colors: Cream, gold, bronze, dark grey, small shades of orange and yellow.
Gemstones: Serpentine.
Offerings: Flight feathers from any bird (found), demonstrations of independence, willingness to do things out of the ordinary.
Prayer: *With wings of uncertainty, I have faith. With joy and velocity, I take flight.*

Crazy Owl Eyes lives in the tangled grove of plum trees and blackberry behind my old house. She will inhabit any sliver of space that is left for wild and thus challenges us to leave well enough alone, to allow the weeds to grow up, the flowers to seed, the stalks to remain, the fruits to return to soil.

Most of us live our lives so far away from wild spaces. Our days are mechanized by clocks and routines, our bodies groomed into submission, our interests combed for their viability in the marketplace. Crazy Owl Eyes says you must be fully yourself in the wild, free of the encumbrances of modern linear thought and gridded living, if you are ever to make rooted decisions, if you are ever to release in joy, if you are ever to truly experience the fullness of life. She invites you to act and imagine without worrying about what other people think, reclaiming the word crazy as a positive affirmation of wild connection and expression.

Dance naked in the moonlight in the yard, drink rainwater from the tips of fir trees, quit your day job and follow your deepest promptings. Nest with her in the wild, see what becomes possible when you stop trying so hard.

notes:

MOTHER MAPLE

Offerings: cover crop seeds and new soil, compost 'round her roots, hours of skygazing through the seasons of her leaves
Prayer: May our wonder grow up through the common.

Mother Maple lives in the enormous cleft tree straddling my yard. Her heart rots daily, the center breaking off in chunks that crumble, and we know she is easily a more than a century old. Her branches though are vast and healthy, holding audiences of tiny clapping leaves in early spring, a canopy of green that frustrates in summer (because my garden gets so little light) but provides a lovely lie-beneath in the fall for watching golden light drift down toward endings.

Crows and flickers are equally nourished by the respite of her branches, squirrels and rats eat the sprouted bounty of her seeds through the winter. One being, one great tree is the provisional resource for multitudes.

She is in my sightline so often I forget to be reverent. This is the way with many spirits in our lives—they vanish at the edge of vision and ask nothing even as they tend daily to our homes, environments, aesthetics.

What spirits of place do you take for granted? Where can you bring the gift of your attention or time? What lessons do you wish for from the enduring presence closest by?

notes:

110

GALA CARDS

The word gala in Old Norse is the root of the word galdr, which means variously song, spell, enchantment or incantation. It is a word used for sacred work, for making magic, and I use it here with that intent.

These three phrases make up one of the most powerful pledges I know. To draw any one is to be reminded of the potency of self-love in our lives.

When we look outside for love and approval, when we give our love to those who hurt us while expecting or wishing for more, we live an imbalance. When we give ourselves love and affection, when we approve of ourselves, and give love to others from a place of self-love, the balance is regained.

If you can give yourself the love you would wish from another, from a parent, a partner, a lover, a friend or a child, you will find a source of strength, power and joy that can never be diminished, that will remain with you always.

(These cards were colored by my daughter, Rhea Madrone, when she was ten.)

= LOVE YOUR BODY =

Your body is beautiful. Right now, as you are, wherever you are. Your body is miraculous, living and breathing, heart beating, cycles cycling. If you drew this card your body might be asking you for some time and attention, for sensory delights such as music, dance, fresh herbs and flowers, sunlight on your skin. Self-care begins with the body, with slowing down and tending to your physical needs. Stretching, walking, naps, slow easy meals of vibrant food, all of these can help frame the Love Your Body card's intent.

Sometimes this card catches you in a place of self-criticism or physical discomfort. It can be helpful to see yourself from the eyes of another, a spirit or being, God, the elements, to view yourself as a whole, a physical part of the world, someone made of earth and stars. That big, that gorgeous, you are.

notes:

LOVE YOUR STORY

The story you tell is the life you live. Stories are a fundamental power, the power of absolute creation. What stories are you telling about yourself right now, your work, the people that surround you, your perceptions on what you should be doing versus what you would like to do? What story would you be living if it was created just by you? And, most importantly, do you love your story right now?

If you do, this card calls for a celebration! If you don't, how can you begin living into the new story you are yearning for, even in small ways? What little pieces of your story do you love, the ones you won't alter no matter what? In the days to come, show those stories appreciation even as you strive to live into something different. Create from a place of absolute expectation, play with what you love most in your imagination. Trust, believe, receive.

notes:

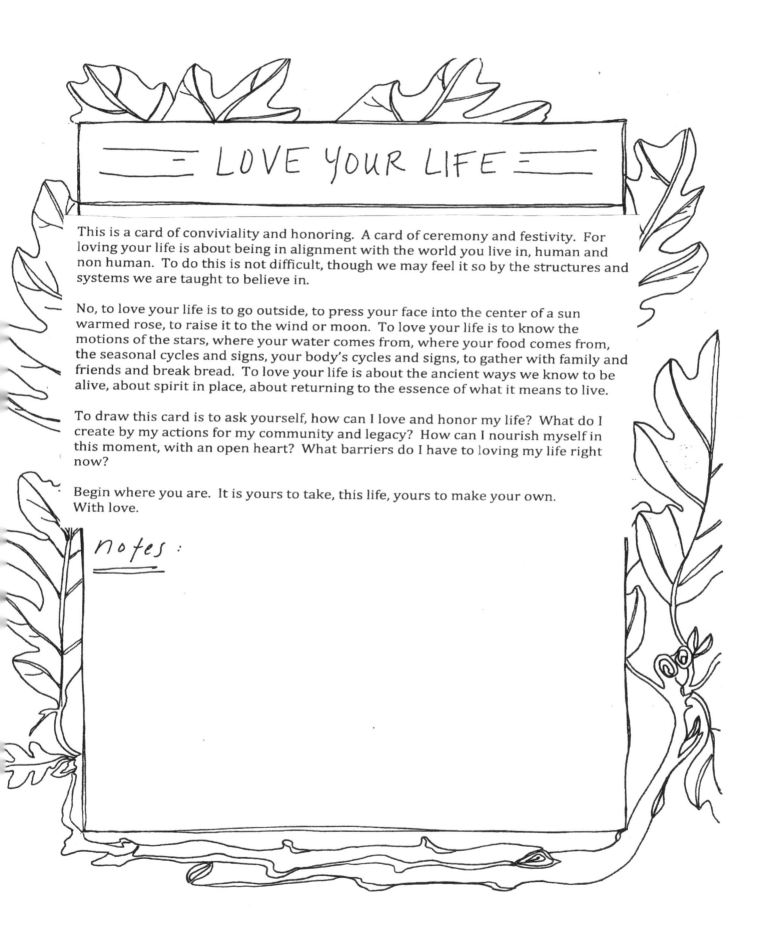

= LOVE YOUR LIFE =

This is a card of conviviality and honoring. A card of ceremony and festivity. For loving your life is about being in alignment with the world you live in, human and non human. To do this is not difficult, though we may feel it so by the structures and systems we are taught to believe in.

No, to love your life is to go outside, to press your face into the center of a sun warmed rose, to raise it to the wind or moon. To love your life is to know the motions of the stars, where your water comes from, where your food comes from, the seasonal cycles and signs, your body's cycles and signs, to gather with family and friends and break bread. To love your life is about the ancient ways we know to be alive, about spirit in place, about returning to the essence of what it means to live.

To draw this card is to ask yourself, how can I love and honor my life? What do I create by my actions for my community and legacy? How can I nourish myself in this moment, with an open heart? What barriers do I have to loving my life right now?

Begin where you are. It is yours to take, this life, yours to make your own. With love.

notes:

A Blessing

May this offering
Bring you comfort
Closeness
Closure
In the circle of your ancestors
guardians and guides
In the web of divine wisdom
In the presence of the whole and holy nature
Of this earth
That you are
May you find your own gifts
Make your own offerings
Open the circle
For another
And so heal the world.
Alu.

Plant Allies and the Sacred Art

Through this book you have been casually introduced to four of my most treasured companions:

- ☆ Quercus garryana — ☆ Oregon white oak
- ☆ Pseudotsuga menziesii — ☆ Douglas fir
- ☆ Daucus carota — ☆ Queen Anne's lace
- ☆ Taraxacum — ☆ Dandelion

Three natives and a naturalized sister whose gifts range from food to shade to antiseptics and contraception. A fundamental tenant of my ever-evolving spirituality is animism. Once, all humans lived in an alive,

...Douglas fir...

animate and participatory universe.
I wish to restore that consciousness.
Thus, the plants are here because
they asked to be. Each spoke to my
heart and through my pen. I love
these beings not for what they can
do, but for who they are. My life
is richer for a reciprocal relationship
with the world around me. We speak,
sing, I make offerings, they give
gifts. In this book they hope to
invite you deeper into the places
where you live, work and play. They
whisper of the solace and joy that
waits just beyond the limits of
human habitation. This world _is_
alive. Remember. We are never alone.
Remember. We belong to each other.
Love.

...Oregon white oak...

WITH GRATITUDE
·· to ···

My partner, Eric, and our children Xavier, Grace and Rhea for their profound patience with my quirks and encouragement of my creative-spirit work. I love you all so very much. My parents, grandparents, brother, sis-in-love, nephew and heroic cousin-crew (helmed by the incredible Rachel) give me roots, nourishment and heart support through the unbelievable adventure of this life. Through this family, I am. Moon Divas everywhere around the globe, you continue to inspire and fill my heart! Women of Magnetize, The Chrysalis Class, The Power Class and the Oracle Circle offered insight, sisterhood and collective imagining to this work. Teachers Ingrid, Marguerite, Shannon, Darlene in PDX; Mara, Anjali, Alka and Afia Walking Tree

—— — continued ——————
—————   Gratitude to   =—

at CIIS in San Francisco: Your wisdom
has shaped and broken and re-formed
my vision and understanding of the
Goddess, of spirituality and healing.
Oh for literature! Oh for new perspectives!
Fellow students of the Women's Spirituality
program, the same and deeper. For
every conversation, I am soul-full.
Last, best & never least: angel of
Moon Divas and the Sacred Creative,
Deva Munay. Your dedication to
this work makes all possible. I am
so happy the book has found a home in
countless brick and mortar shops thanks
to your natural, effortful distribution.
Here's to the symbiosis of making:
we never, ever are in this alone...
Love! And to you, reader, taking a
risk on the handmade-small. Blessings,
sweetness, joy.

This Book Was Made at Home: Embracing Imperfection

There are tape marks, smudges, specks of dust from the scanner. All attest to the same tale: this book was drawn, written and lovingly assembled in my home. There are errors, inconsistencies and repetitions. Again: the story I live is here. Much like The Moon Divas Guidebook, this creation and its cards would not be possible if I waited for perfection (or a publisher... or a computer that will run Photoshop). If the choice is between sharing our beautiful, messy, dusty-smudged sacred gifts or holding on for some sanitized version, I choose to <u>make</u> and <u>share</u> in the service of spirits who whirl through the intricacies and eschew linearity. May it be an altar, may it inspire you to show your truth.

ABOUT LARA

photo credit: Lorijo Daniels

I am an artist and writer working at the intersection of image and word. My interests include folk spirituality, ancestral mythology, ritual and the sacred creative. I'm the author of *The Moon Divas Guidebook: Spirited Self-Care for Women in Transition* (2012) and illustrator for *The Runes Revealed* (2016). I practice under the name Veleda Vesta, in part to raise awareness about women's historical relationship with natural divination and oracular power.

To learn more and weave webs: laravesta.co
Instagram: @veledavesta

REFLECTION

DREAMING

INSPIRATION

CREATIVITY

☆ Your ☆ Reading Record and Notes . . . .

reading record ... date ... moon ....

...reading record... date... moon.............

reading record ... date ... moon ....

reading record... date... moon...........

...reading record... date... moon..........